MW01243511

AMERICAN HISTORY

VOLUME VI: THE REVOLT OF THE COLONIES

JACOB ABBOTT

SANDYCROFT PUBLISHING

American History Vol. VI: The Revolt of the Colonies

By Jacob Abbott

First published 1864

This edition ©2014

Sandycroft Publishing

http://sandycroftpublishing.com

ISBN 978-1500651312

CONTENTS

CHAPTER III
THE STAMP ACT

CHAPTER IV
PROGRESS OF THE QUARREL

CHAPTER V
MILITARY PREPARATIONS

CHAPTER VI
THE MIDDLE AND SOUTHERN COLONIES

CHAPTER VII
THE BOSTON MASSACRE

CHAPTER VIII
POPULAR OUTBREAKS

CHAPTER IX
THE BOSTON PORT BILL

CHAPTER X
War

LIST OF ENGRAVINGS

PREFACE

It is the design of this work to narrate, in a clear, simple, and intelligible manner, the leading events connected with the history of our country, from the earliest periods, down, as nearly as practicable, to the present time. The several volumes will be illustrated with all necessary maps and with numerous engravings, and the work is intended to comprise, in a distinct and connected narrative, all that it is essential for the general reader to understand in respect to the subject of it, while for those who have time for more extended studies, it may serve as an introduction to other and more copious sources of information.

The author hopes also that the work may be found useful to the young, in awakening in their minds an interest in the history of their country, and a desire for further instruction in respect to it. While it is doubtless true that such a subject can be really grasped only by minds in some degree mature, still the author believes that many young persons, especially such as are intelligent and thoughtful in disposition and character, may derive both entertainment and instruction from a perusal of these pages.

Encampment on Boston Common.

THE REVOLT OF THE COLONIES

CHAPTER I
PRINCIPLES OF GOVERNMENT

DIVERGENCY OF EUROPEAN AND AMERICAN IDEAS

In order to clearly understand the origin and the character of the difficulties between the American colonies and the mother country, which led to the revolt of the colonies against the English authorities, and finally to the establishment of their independence, it is necessary to consider the vast difference between the ideas and doctrines in respect to the nature of human government which were gradually formed in the minds of the people of this country, during the continuance of the colonial condition, and which came at last universally to prevail on this side of the Atlantic, and those which had been handed down from generation to generation in Europe, and which, at that period, held universal sway in the old world. It was, in a great measure, out of this difference of view that the early dissensions between the colonies and the parent government originated, and it was, perhaps, wholly owing to it that the difficulty became in the end irreconcilable, and that a system of government was at length inaugurated in America, so radically different, in its fundamental principles from the hereditary systems of the old world.

THE NATURAL ORIGIN OF GOVERNMENT

Among a flock or herd of gregarious animals, the strongest takes the command, and constitutes himself the monarch. This is the intention of nature. If it is doubtful which of two or more individuals is the strongest, they fight each other until the question is determined, and when one proves his superiority, the rest acknowledge his right to reign. This, too, seems to be the intention of nature, in respect

1

to the organization and government of those vast communities of beasts and birds which are found banded together, in a state of nature, in various regions of the earth and the air.

Something very analogous to this seems to prevail when we take a step upward in the scale of animated nature, in going from flocks and herds of beasts to tribes of savage men. In these, too, the strongest assumes the command—there being included now, however, among the elements of strength, not merely muscular and physical power—but sagacity, and other means of acquiring moral ascendancy over the minds of ordinary men. Still, it is *strength,* in this case as well as in the other, that constitutes the right to reign. The man who—all things considered—is best *able* to command, assumes the right to command. If there is a question which of two or more individuals is best able, that is, which is really the strongest, a combat settles the question, and the community acquiesces in the result.

No Other Government Possible in the Early Stages of Society

Even if we cannot decide it to be the intention of nature that in a barbarous state of society the strongest should rule, we can, at any rate, say that so far as we can see, no other government, in such a state of things, is possible. Philosophically, and of just right, the *general will* of the *community,* whether in a herd of beasts, a flock of birds, or a tribe of savage men, is the will that ought to govern; but in such communities there is no way of ascertaining the general will, nor of embodying it in any such form as to give it practical effect. Until, therefore, the community to be governed makes such advances in intelligence, and in power of organization, as to bring the general will to its proper ascendancy, the will of the strongest, that is, of the individual best able to regulate, control and protect, must govern, or there must be anarchy.

Accordingly in all parts of the world and among all nations, in looking back to early ages we find that human communities, at the time of their emergence from the ages of darkness and barbarism into the light of history, come into view organized under some form or other of monarchical or aristocratic government—the rulers holding their authority, not in any sense from the will of the people, but solely by virtue of the power exercised by themselves, or by their ancestors, in seizing and retaining it.

Nature and Origin of the Civil Liberties Enjoyed by the People in Europe

In process of time, as civilization and the arts advanced, the people of the various countries of Europe did indeed succeed in curtailing the power of their hereditary rulers, and in securing certain rights and privileges, and, in the end, some actual share in the government, for themselves; but these rights and privileges were almost always gained, and they are still held, by the people of these nations, as *grants* and concessions from their sovereigns, and not as inherent rights originating in themselves.

In other words the idea in respect to human government which has always prevailed and still holds sway in a greater or less extent in all the countries of Europe, is that it is a power *above* the people—supreme—sovereign, and having an origin that ascends to so remote an antiquity that its authority is not to be questioned or inquired into, even if it is not to be considered as absolutely divine.

American Ideas of Government

The ideas in respect to the proper origin and true nature of governmental power that prevail in this country are radically different from these. Government is now, and always has been, in this country, considered as a species of agency, exercised by the will and at the pleasure of the principals, the people, and the power which a government wields is regarded as not by any means held in its own right, but by special grant from the people who have constituted it, and may be modified, enlarged, abridged, or entirely annulled, at the pleasure of those for whose benefit it was conferred and is to be exercised.

Thus according to the ideas of the old world the rights of the people are considered in some sense as grants conferred upon them by government which reigns supreme through a sort of inherent sovereignty that it has held from time immemorial. Whereas in the new, it is the power of the government which is held as a grant, the rights of the people being inherent and supreme, and the government being possessed of no power but such as they hold *from* the people and during their pleasure.

CAUSE OF THIS DIVERSITY

It is very easy to perceive the cause of this diversity in the systems that prevail on the two continents. The nations of the old world emerged from barbarism as communities already organized under the government of the strongest, the organization being made continuous by the principle of hereditary descent of power—a principle which is not only the most important element of strength for those claiming the right to reign among savage and half civilized tribes, but the only one by which a constant succession of bloody struggles and consequent anarchy can be avoided, in cases where the people are not far advanced enough in intelligence and means of combination to give peaceful effect to their united will. The power therefore of one royal or many noble families, or of both, comes down in all these nations from very ancient times, in a condition of firm and permanent establishment, and the people are taught that this power is held of right, and even by divine institution, and that they must submit to it implicitly; and in respect to their own rights and privileges be content with such grants and concessions as these their natural superiors may deem it safe from time to time to confer upon them.

ORIGIN OF GOVERNMENT IN AMERICA

On the other hand the exercise of governmental power and the organization of the community into a body politic had a very different origin in America. The first companies of emigrants that came to form settlements in America brought with them no germs of the aristocratic and hereditary systems of the old world. The Plymouth party for example came as a company of equals, with only a spiritual organization as a church, and this of a purely democratic character. They left England, and crossed the Atlantic, so far as their worldly interests were concerned, as so many independent men, each one responsible for taking care of himself and his family, and none of them having any right or authority, hereditary or otherwise, to exercise jurisdiction over the rest. Just before they landed, they met together, and drew up articles of agreement in which they constituted their company a body politic for the better management of certain interests common to them all. They thus constituted a species of governmental authority which they clothed with certain specified powers, which powers were to be held and exercised solely for the benefit of the grantors, and within the limits which the grantors assigned to them.

A great many of the first companies of settlers that came to America were left in this manner entirely to themselves for a considerable period, and they severally proceeded to frame from time to time such rules and regulations as they found necessary for the common safety, each member of the community having an equal voice, and the safety and welfare of the individual members being the sole end and aim of the organization, and the measure and limit of the power conferred on the authorities constituted by the act. Such simple machinery as this was hardly to be considered as a government. It was at first rather the constitution of a partnership than the organization of a state; but it was all the government that was needed, and as it gradually enlarged itself and became more complicated, as the settlements increased and extended, the successive generations of men came into it, one after another, and grew up in it with the understanding that government was of the nature of an agency, constituted by the people, and in all respects directly amenable to them.

THE PROPRIETARY GOVERNMENTS

There was something in a certain degree analogous to the old world system, that is the system of governments originating from *above* the people, and acting downward upon them, in what were called the proprietary colonies. In these, as is more fully explained in former volumes of this series, wealthy men in England obtained grants from the king of large tracts of land in America, and then made arrangements with families of settlers to come out and occupy them, they, namely the proprietors, reserving to themselves certain powers in respect to the government of the colonies thus established. But in these cases the practical result always was that even from the outset the principal control of public affairs was soon assumed by the settlers themselves, and in process of time, the proprietors, after vainly struggling to retain their proper share of power, were in all cases obliged to relinquish it altogether, and the democratic principle of government by the *power of the whole,* and for the benefit of the whole, reigned supreme.

EARLY INDIFFERENCE OF THE MOTHER COUNTRY IN RESPECT TO THE COLONIES

For some time after the first settlements in America were made, the people who formed them were left pretty much to themselves, and allowed to manage their affairs in their own way, as described in the preceding paragraphs. The government in England seemed not to consider the infant states of enough consequence to make it worthwhile to attempt to secure any great control over them. The government, in fact, whenever it did interpose, acted apparently without any regard to the welfare of the colonies themselves, but only with a view to the interest, for the time being, of the mother country, or rather for that of the kingly power which ruled over it. Sometimes they encouraged emigration, when they thought the effect of it would be to take out of the kingdom certain turbulent and refractory spirits that they could not very well manage in it. Then afterward when they found that a class of persons were going to America that were profitable to the community in England, they restricted or forbade emigration. When they found that the territory in America began to be considered as possessing a certain money value, they made grants of it to their friends and favorites, either to individual personages of distinction, in payment of debts incurred for past services, or to companies of merchants formed for the purpose, and who paid for the acquisition a stipulated sum.

Increasing Importance of the Colonies

In a few years more, as the settlements increased, and began to acquire some importance, and especially as the commercial intercourse with the colonies—the conveying of the products which they raised, to Europe, and the carrying back, from Europe, products and manufactures in return—began to be profitable, the attention of the king and his ministers was turned more particularly toward these rising communities, and they began to show a greater inclination to assume some control in the management of their affairs. Thus there came to be three parties that were more or less interested in the government of the colonies, namely, the king's government in England, the proprietors or grantees of the territory, who claimed rights and powers conferred upon them by the grants they held, and the people themselves.

Conflicting Claims

The conflicting claims of these parties led to a great many disputes and to much contention. These disputes were terminated at one time in one colony and at another time in another, by the issuing of what was called a royal charter, which was a very formal and solemn document, drawn up on parchment and authenticated with ponderous seals and other official formalities, which prescribed precisely the respective powers of the people of the colonies, and of the royal government, in respect to the management of their affairs.

Royal Charters

By these charters the inhabitants of the colonies were usually empowered to elect a legislature, and through this legislature to enact all laws and to make all rules and regulations for the internal government of the respective communities. The king of England, on the other hand, retained what is called the executive administration, as his own prerogative. He, or his ministers in his names, reserved the right to appoint the governor of the colony, and the judges who were to preside in the courts. The governor thus appointed by him was made commander-in-chief of such troops as should be sent to the colony from time to time, whether to garrison towns and fortresses in time of peace, or to conduct military operations in time of war.

Thus in general terms it may be said that the management of the internal affairs of each community, and the regulation of the rights and duties of individuals in the ordinary relations of life, were committed to the people themselves, while the whole control of the colony considered as an organized power, was retained in the hands of the king.

CONFLICTS UNDER THE CHARTER GOVERNORS

The granting of a charter to a colony was by no means sure to put an end to all conflicts in respect to the government of it. The governor appointed by the king and sent out from England, and the officers of the army, holding commissions directly from him, came out to the colonies to which they were sent, entertaining usually very lofty ideas of their importance, as in a certain sense the direct representatives of sovereignty. They were the depositories of power coming from above downward, and in no sense responsible to those below them. They looked down with a feeling of condescension when they were in good humor, and of contempt when in bad, upon provincial assemblies composed of men who derived their powers from the mass of the people, and were directly responsible to them for the exercise of it. In a word the governors, the judges, and the military officers in the colonies, represented the aristocratic and monarchical principle, and acted always in the interest of the royal government at home. On the other hand the principle embodied in the legislative assemblies was democratic, and the interest which they represented was that of the people of the colony. Hence continual collisions and conflicts occurred, in which royal power and prerogative maintained by the governor, the judges, and the military men, struggled against the rights and privileges claimed by the people.

CONTESTS IN RESPECT TO THE CHARTERS

The contests between the crown, acting chiefly through the British ministers, and the royal governors who represented the crown in America on the one hand, and the people of the colonies on the other, often turned on the interpretation of the charters, and sometimes on the validity of them. Each party claimed under the charter, greater powers or privileges than the other allowed, and when any colony made such claims and acted upon them, the ministry would sometimes declare that the charter was forfeited, and would demand of the colonial authorities the surrender of it, or they would institute proceedings in the courts of law, with a view to having it declared null and void. In some cases the governor of a colony would undertake to annul a charter or to demand the surrender of it, and in one instance, in the case of Connecticut, a remarkable occurrence took place, which subsequently became quite famous in the history of that state.

The Charter Oak at Hartford

The incident occurred in the year 1685, in the reign of King James the Second. This monarch entertained very exalted ideas of the kingly power and prerogative, and considered society as prosperous and safe just in proportion as the lower classes, by which was meant the great mass of the community, were obedient and submissive to the authorities divinely constituted to rule over them. He was much dissatisfied with the loose manner in which the colonies had been managed by the government of his predecessor, Charles the Second, who had encouraged the settlers to assume gradually a degree of control in public affairs, which he and his ministers judged wholly inconsistent with the principles of good government. He accordingly commissioned and sent out to America an energetic man, named Andros, with instructions to reform these abuses, and reduce the colonists to their proper state of submission.

The powers conferred upon Governor Andros extended over all the New England colonies. He commenced his operations in Boston, and while engaged there in bringing the Massachusetts and Plymouth colonies to terms, he wrote to the magistrates of the colony of Connecticut that their charter had been forfeited, and must be surrendered, and directed them to send it to him. This order the magistrates disregarded, and at length, after the lapse of some months,

Progress of the royal governor.

Andros proceeded to Hartford in great state, being accompanied by a large suite of attendants and followers, and an escort of troops for a bodyguard. At Hartford, he came into the assembly, which was at that time in session, and demanded that the charter should be given up to him. The governor of the colony, in reply to this demand, made a speech, in which he strongly urged the injustice of depriving the colony of their charter. He represented the great expense which the colonists had incurred, and the hardships they had endured, in founding the colony, and the blood and treasure which they had expended in defending it, both against savages and foreigners. He alluded particularly to the hardships to which he himself had been exposed, and the toil and suffering he had endured—and added, that it was now like giving up his life to surrender the patent and privileges which had been so dearly bought and so long enjoyed.

PROGRESS OF THE ROYAL GOVERNOR

By this speech, and by the debate in the assembly, and the other proceedings which followed, the affair was kept in suspense until the evening, by which time a large number of people had assembled. The charter itself had been brought in and laid upon the table of the house, awaiting the action of the assembly in surrendering it, as demanded by Andros, and during the interval a plot, it seems, was formed to convey it away and conceal it, in order to prevent its falling into Andros's hands.

THE CHARTER DISAPPEARS

Accordingly, at a concerted signal, the lights were suddenly put out, and then the whole room immediately became a scene of confusion. Some of the people began at once with great pretended eagerness and alacrity to light the candles again—taking care, however, to allow time for the others to convey the charter away. As soon as the lights reappeared the charter was gone. For a long time very few persons knew what had become of it.

Andros immediately declared the existing government of the colony at an end. He brought the records of the assembly to a close by an entry therein, saying that thenceforth he took the control of the colony into his own hands, and annexed it to Massachusetts and to the other colonies which were under his government.

He, accordingly, immediately assumed a sort of sovereign power over all the colonies of New England. But the state of things thus introduced did not long continue, for King James, by the revolution of 1688, lost his throne; and this change in the mother country was followed by a revolution in America by which Andros was deposed, and the several colonies which he had attempted to unite under his own control, returned to their former condition.

THE CHARTER OAK

The charter of Connecticut was then brought to light again, and it now became known that it had been concealed in a hollow in the trunk of an oak that grew near the house of one of the magistrates. The cavity in which it was hidden was near the bottom of the trunk, and was large enough, as is stated in the annals of those days, "to contain a child."

This tree became, of course, in subsequent years, an object of great historical interest. It was called the Charter Oak, and it remained standing after this time for about one hundred and seventy years. Indeed, it seems in some measure to have improved in condition as it advanced in years, for the opening in which the charter was concealed entirely disappeared from view. It was, however, closed by the growth of a thin, superficial layer of wood, which concealed only, but did not remedy, the decay and hollowness within. Thus the apparent health and strength of the stem, as it presented itself to the eyes of visitors, was unreal, and at length, in August, 1856, the tree was blown down in a violent storm. A portion of the wood was employed to make a frame for the ancient charter, and in this frame the venerable document is still preserved in the office of the Secretary of State at Hartford. The rest of the wood was manufactured into canes, boxes, carved ornaments, and other objects of art, which were at once highly prized by all interested in the early history of New England, and have since been widely distributed throughout the country.

This famous charter constituted the fundamental law of Connecticut for more than a hundred years. It was at length superseded by the adoption of the present constitution of the state, in the year 1818.

CHAPTER II
THE MOTHER COUNTRY AND THE COLONIES

RELATION OF THE COLONIES TO THE MOTHER COUNTRY

In the conflict of jurisdiction, in respect to the government of the American colonies, between the colonies themselves on the one side, and the king and Parliament of Great Britain on the other, there were four principal points in regard to which the parties came most frequently and most earnestly into collision. By considering these special subjects of controversy a little in detail, the reader will be enabled to form a pretty clear idea of the nature and the progress of the difficulty, which ended in the American revolution. These four points, representing claims made by the British and disallowed and resisted from time to time, with more or less of earnestness, by the colonies, were the following.

THE FOUR GREAT SUBJECTS OF CONTENTION

1. The English government claimed the exclusive right to regulate and control the whole *foreign trade and commerce of the colonies.*

2. They claimed that the judges in all the colonial courts should be not only appointed by the king, that is by the home government, but that they should hold office not permanently, but only during the king's pleasure, thus making them wholly dependent on his will.

3. That the governors too should not only be appointed by the king or his ministers, but should also be made

independent of the colonies by having a permanent salary settled upon them.

4. That besides the control of the foreign commerce of the colonies, Parliament had also the right of *internal taxation*, in respect to them—that is the right to levy taxes upon the people themselves directly, as they were accustomed to do upon the people of England.

These claims were the four great points in dispute between the colonies and the parent state, and they continued to be, in a greater or less degree, subjects of contention during the whole colonial period. In regard to the first, the decision was practically in favor of the government, for the colonies, though they would not acknowledge the justice of the claim of the English to regulate their commerce, could not resist it, and consequently this commerce was, in fact, from the beginning, subject entirely to the trade and navigation laws of Great Britain.

In regard to the second and third points, namely, those relating to the tenure of office of the judges, and the salaries of the governors, the question was never fully and finally settled, but remained in controversy—the various disputes to which it gave rise, leading to different results in different colonies and at different times. There were endless negotiations, and maneuvers, and compromises, and temporary victories of one side or the other, but no general and final settlement was ever attained.

In respect to the last—the right of the home government to assess internal taxes—the colonies were destined to gain the day. The government made vigorous and determined efforts to enforce their claim, but these efforts led to revolt, and finally to revolution.

But we must consider these several points a little more in detail.

1.—THE RIGHT OF THE GOVERNMENT TO REGULATE THE COMMERCE OF THE COLONIES

The government claimed that the Parliament, being the supreme legislature of England, could justly regulate the trade and commerce of all parts of the empire, and this they proceeded to do, at a very early period in the history of the colonies, by what were called the Trade and Navigation acts. For some time the colonies scarcely called this right in question, though the system which was adopted in the exercise of it was very onerous to them. This was the colonial system, as it was called, as adopted in those days by almost all the nations of Europe that possessed colonies in any of the other quarters of the globe.

THE COLONIAL SYSTEM

The colonial system generally adopted by the European nations in those days, was this, that no colony could have any commercial intercourse with the rest of the world except *through the mother country.* This was in fact one of the chief advantages, as it was thought, in possessing colonies, namely, that thereby the trade and commerce of the mother country might be enlarged, and the merchants and navigators enriched. Accordingly a series of acts were passed from time to time by the British Parliament, the end and aim of which were to provide that all the trade and commerce of the colonies should be conducted exclusively in English ships, commanded by English captains and manned chiefly by English sailors. No goods could be introduced into the colonies, no matter in what countries they were produced, except *through English merchants,* and none of the chief productions of the colonies could be sent to any other country than England.

DOUBLE OBJECT TO BE SECURED BY THIS SYSTEM

There were two objects which the European nations intended to secure by the adoption of this system—for substantially the same policy was pursued by France, Spain and other European nations, in respect to their colonies. The first was to enrich their own merchants by giving them a monopoly of the trade, and the second to increase the number of seamen in the merchant service from which the government could draw recruits in time of war. If England, for example, prohibited all other nations from trading with her colonies, but required all ships entering their ports to be officered and manned mainly by Englishmen, the number of English sailors that would become trained to the sea would be vastly increased, and the sailors would be available to man the national vessels in time of war.

Now the obtaining of men is one of the greatest difficulties to be encountered in the attempt of any nation to create a powerful navy. A ship can be built and equipped in a year, and for land operations, soldiers can be trained and disciplined in six months. But to make *sailors*—men who can work coolly on a lofty yard, a hundred feet above a boiling and roaring sea, standing upon a rope that is swaying to and fro under their feet, and supporting themselves with one hand while they hold their iron grip upon an inflexible rope or a stiff and unmanageable sail with the other, requires many years of experience at sea, an experience too which must be begun in early life. Seamen therefore cannot be extemporized, and all nations who aim at being powerful at sea, feel it to be necessary so to shape their legislation as to create a great mercantile marine, in time of peace, so as to have a sufficient maritime population to draw from in time of war.

This was, doubtless, one great object which the British government had in view, in confining all the trade and commerce of the colonies to English vessels.

The Colonies Unable to Resist the English Navigation Laws

Although at various times, and in different ways, the colonists made many complaints, and sometimes offered earnest remonstrances against the restrictions thus imposed upon their intercourse with the world, by the English system, they were utterly helpless in respect to making any resistance to it. The English government was supreme upon the seas, while they themselves possessed no naval power whatever. The ports of America were, consequently, entirely under the command of English guns, and all intercourse and communication with them, both of access and egress, was under English control. There was nothing, therefore, for the colonies to do but to submit.

2.—THE TENURE OF OFFICE IN THE CASE OF JUDGES

The English government desired to make the judges that presided in the colonial courts directly responsible to the crown, by giving to the king the power of removing them and appointing others at his pleasure. The colonists, on the other hand, wished to have them, when once appointed, wholly independent, by securing them in office for life, provided they faithfully performed their duties. A great many cases were likely to occur, in which political questions would come before the judges—cases in which the rights and privileges of the people came in conflict with the powers of government, or the prerogatives of the crown. There could be no security for an impartial decision in such cases if the king could at any time dismiss a judge from office and appoint another in his place. Whereas, if the office once conferred were permanent, the judge would be far less exposed to any temptation to swerve from a just judgment in order to please the supreme power. An independent judiciary, the colonists claimed, was the only safeguard of the rights of the people against the usurpations of governmental power.

A great many different contentions arose from time to time in the different colonies in respect to this question, sometimes one side and sometimes the other gaining a local and temporary advantage, but without any final or satisfactory result.

3.—THE SALARIES OF THE GOVERNORS

While the English government were very earnest in their desires and efforts to keep the judges dependent on the king, and thus subservient to his will, they were equally active in their efforts to prevent the governors being held in any way under responsibility to the people of the colonies. The king's government in England appointed the governors, but the colonies paid their salaries. The government wished their salaries to be made *permanent,* so that the proper officers could pay them each year, as they became due, without any new grant from the legislature. The colonies, on the other hand, wished to make only *annual grants* for the governor's salary, so as to put him under some obligation to manage public affairs in such a manner as to give satisfaction to the people, for fear that if he did not do so, the legislature would make difficulty about voting his salary. And at any rate, such an arrangement would necessarily lead to bringing the governor himself and the principles of his administration, under discussion every year in the assembly, when the question of making the appropriation for his salary came up. But this was considered in England as subjecting the governor to a great indignity, and, moreover, it tended to bring him under a species of direct responsibility to the people wholly inconsistent with the ideas which prevailed among the monarchies of Europe in respect to the proper relations which should subsist between the rulers and the ruled.

THE MODERATION OF THE CLAIM MADE BY THE COLONIES

This question in regard to the governors was, in some sense, analogous to that in relation to the judges, the aim of the king being in both cases to keep the officers in question directly and continually responsible to him alone. He had already the appointment of the judges in his own hands, and he wished also to have the power of dismissing them. In respect to the governors, he had already both the power of appointing and dismissing them, as the governors confessedly held their offices only during the king's pleasure, and he wished to make his power over them absolute and exclusive, by requiring that the salaries which they were to receive from the people should be fixed and permanent, so as to take away from the colonies all power of effectually opposing his administration, even when they thought it unjust or oppressive.

That is to say, the king wished to exclude the colonies entirely from the exercise of any influence over either class of officers, and to make his own influence complete and absolute over both.

The colonies, on the other hand, did not claim any exclusive or absolute power for themselves. In respect to the judges, they claimed nothing for themselves, but only that those officers, once appointed, should be left free to act as their own sense of justice might dictate. And in regard to the governor, they only claimed for themselves a very limited and partial control over him. They were willing to allow the crown to appoint the governor, but, as an offset to that power, they wished that when appointed he should acknowledge some indirect and limited responsibility to the people over whom he ruled.

4.—The Power of Direct Taxation

The first of the four great matters of difference between the English government and the colonies, namely, the right to regulate trade and commerce, includes, as is evident, the right of what is called *indirect* taxation, that is, the laying and collecting duties on merchandise imported into the country. These duties are paid by the merchant or importer at the custom-house, when the goods are landed, and the amount which the merchant has thus to pay, he of course adds to the price of the goods when he sells them to the people. Thus the merchant pays in the first instance, and is afterward reimbursed by his customers. The people thus pay *indirectly*.

Direct taxation, on the other hand, consists in a levy of a certain sum or sums upon each individual of the community, according to the amount or kind of property he holds, or to the employment which he follows, or to his income, and is collected *directly* of each individual by the tax gatherers of the government.

The English government claimed the right of taxing the colonies in both these ways.

The Result, in Practice

Although the government claimed the right of both indirect and direct taxation, the practical result was, that during almost the whole colonial period, the first right was exercised by them, and the latter was not. For a long time, the population of the settlements was so small, and the amount of property possessed by the inhabitants was so insignificant, that any internal tax would have produced very little revenue, while the expense and difficulty of collecting it would have been very great. In respect to duties on imported merchandise, the case was different. Such a tax as that is very easily collected, as it is paid at once in large sums by the merchant or importer before the goods really enter the country. The work of collecting the several amounts from individual consumers is thrown upon the merchants, who get back, in detail, the duties they have paid in the gross, by adding the amount to the price of the goods, thus saving the government all trouble.

Then, besides, the people are much more easily induced to pay a tax of this kind, which is, as it were, concealed from their view by being merged in the purchase money of an article they require, than they are to submit to a *direct* taxation in any form, to the same amount. Half the people do not really understand the operation of the system, and those who do understand it, and who remonstrate against it, find it very difficult, in most cases, to awaken in the minds of the rest, any very decided opposition to an evil so hidden from their view. The consequence was, in practice, that the British government adopted the principle of *indirect* taxation of the colonies by restrictions on the commerce, and by duties on imports, at a very early period; and the colonies submitted to the imposts thus made with very little remonstrance.

On the other hand, though the government claimed an equal *right* to levy direct taxes, they did not attempt for a long time to exercise the right, on account of the small return which could be expected, considered in relation to the difficulty, expense and opposition which the attempt would occasion.

THE TIME FOR DIRECT TAXATION ARRIVES

At length however the time arrived when the British government deemed it expedient for them to assume their long dormant right to raise a revenue from the colonies by direct taxation. They were led to this conclusion by the growing greatness and wealth of the colonies, taken in connection with the increasing expenses of the mother country, arising from the enormously costly wars in which she had been engaged. The conquest of Canada too seems to have had a great influence upon them. So long as the French held their possessions in North America the British were somewhat cautious in their treatment of their own colonies, not knowing to what complications any disagreement between the colonies and the mother country might lead. But when at last Canada fell into their hands, and thus they obtained secure possession of the whole country, and every fortress and stronghold throughout the whole extent of it was garrisoned by their troops, and all the ports occupied and commanded by their ships of war, they thought the time had come for them to assume that supreme civil and political authority over the colonies which they contended the central government had a right to exercise over all the provinces of the empire.

GROUNDS OF RESISTANCE ON THE PART OF THE COLONIES

The colonists were prepared to resist this claim, and the ground of their resistance was this—not that they objected to be taxed in their fair proportion, to raise money for the general expenses of the empire—but only that they claimed that the assessing and collecting these taxes should be left to their own legislatures, and not be under the control of the Parliament of England. They grounded their claim to determine for themselves the amount that they would pay, and to decide upon the mode in which the amount should be collected, on certain inherent and indefeasible rights vested in every Englishman, according to the principles of the British constitution.

THEORY OF THE BRITISH CONSTITUTION

According to the principles of the British constitution it is in theory the inherent and indefeasible right of the king to govern the country without any dictation or control from the people. And it is the inherent and indefeasible right of the people, meaning by the people that portion of them that are represented in the House of Commons—to pay, or withhold, the expense of such government, just as they please, without any dictation or control from the king.

PRACTICAL OPERATION OF THE SYSTEM

The practical operation of this system is excellent—I mean in a democratic sense—for it really transfers the power to the people. The king's own personal means for providing for the expenses of government are very limited. He can do nothing unless he is supplied with revenues in some way from his subjects. Now if he is deprived of all power of raising revenues himself, and is dependent entirely upon the action of the people for the assessments made, his hands are completely tied. He can carry on the government only so far as the people—meaning always in the case of England that portion of the people that are represented in the House of Commons—approve of his measures and vote the funds for carrying them into effect.

Thus, for example, the king of England may declare war whenever he pleases, but he can have no ships built, to enable him to pass over to the enemy's country, and no provisions purchased to supply the armies, unless the House of Commons furnish the supplies. Thus while the right of making war rests, in theory, with the king, the absolute control of his decision rests with the House of Commons.

Even in respect to the ordinary legislation of the realm, the theory of the constitution originally was that Parliament is an advisory body only, called together by the king to give him their counsel in respect to such questions as he should lay before them, and to mature the details of measures which he should indicate as desirable. Even to this day an act of Parliament takes the form, not of a law enacted by the two houses, but of a *recommendation to the king* of a law for *him* to enact.

This, however, though it might have been very different originally, is in the present age of the world merely a matter of form. The actual power of the British Parliament in controlling the administration of public affairs, both external and internal, is as complete as that of any legislative assembly in the world. The important thing to be observed is that Parliament holds this power, not directly, and as a matter of theory and form, but *indirectly* and *contrary* to the theory and the form, through the *power which it claims of granting or withholding the supplies.*

WATCHFUL JEALOUSY OF ENGLISHMEN IN RESPECT TO THIS POWER

It is very natural that, since this control over the revenues to be raised by taxation, constitutes almost the sole hold which the people of the country have over a government which would otherwise be irresponsible and supreme, they should be very tenacious of the right, and very jealous of any encroachments upon it. This has accordingly always been the case. This question of taxation and the supplies has in fact been the arena on which have been fought nearly all the conflicts between the crown and the people in England, for centuries. The people in the end have entirely gained the day. And though the old forms still remain, giving the power ostensibly to the king, the actual control has passed entirely into the hands of the people. The king of England no longer governs. The person of the sovereign serves a very important purpose as the visible badge and emblem of the national unity, and the point of concentration and support for the national loyalty; but his opinions and wishes, in respect to the management of public affairs, are no longer of any account. The people—meaning still always, that portion of them that are represented in the House of Commons—by controlling the ways and means, control the policy, and their right to do so they consider as the great inherent and indefeasible political right of an Englishman.

FEELING OF THE AMERICAN COLONISTS

It was natural that the emigrants to the settlements in America should bring with them these ideas, and that they should attempt to give effect to them in the institutions which grew up under their direction and control in the new world. Accordingly in all the colonial governments taxes were levied, and grants of money were made, by the legislative assemblies which were chosen by the people, and the royal governors, though they commanded the troops, and administered the whole executive power, were very strictly precluded from exercising any function whatever, connected with the raising of money. And now when the news came from England that the British ministry were going to bring forward a measure in Parliament, for a general taxation of the colonies by parliamentary authority, it excited among them universal indignation and alarm. They began earnestly to complain, taking the ground that it was wholly inconsistent with the time-honored principles of the British constitution that freeborn Englishmen should be taxed by a legislative authority which they had no voice in electing.

ARGUMENT OF THE BRITISH WRITERS

The argument of the British writers in reply to this claim, was that though it was true that British subjects could not be taxed except by themselves or their representatives, it was not necessary that these representatives should be actually chosen by them. It was only a small portion of the actual population of England that had the privilege of voting for members of Parliament, and yet the taxes voted by Parliament were binding on the whole. Those who did not vote were *virtually* represented, they said. A certain portion of the people of England elected the Parliament. The Parliament, when thus elected however, *represented* the whole, and were authorized to act for them, and to bind them. The people of the colonies were in this respect in precisely the same condition with those portions of the home population which had no voice in choosing the members of Parliament. They were *virtually* represented. In other words the British constitution prescribed a mode in which by the action of a portion of the people a legislative body was chosen, which, when chosen, represented the whole population of the empire, including those inhabiting remote and foreign colonies, as well as those that remained in their native land.

THE REPLY OF THE COLONISTS TO THIS ARGUMENT

To this the colonists replied, that if the people of England who did not vote for members of Parliament might be considered in any sense as represented in the Parliament, it could only be because their interests were the same with those who did vote, and thus these interests were sure to be considered; and also because the taxation decided upon by the Parliament affected the non-voting portion of the people just as it did their immediate constituents—the voting portion—so that they could not do injustice to one class without doing the same injustice to the other. In both these respects the case of the colonists was entirely different. Their interests were not in any degree the same with those of the people of England, nor was the system of taxation to be the same. There could thus be no security that their interests would be properly considered in Parliament since there were none of the members of that body, or of their constituents, that shared those interests; nor any guarantee against their being oppressively taxed, since those who were to vote the taxes would not, either in themselves or by their constituents, be in any way affected by them. Consequently, however it might be with the non-voting portion of the people of England, they themselves, the colonists maintained, were not even *virtually* represented in the English Parliament.

A Real Representation of the Colonies in Parliament Proposed

An obvious remedy for the difficulty of the colonies not being represented in Parliament would be to allow them to elect a certain number of members to that body, and this plan was proposed, and was to some extent seriously considered. But it was not acceptable to either party. In the first place it was wholly inconsistent with the conceptions entertained in England of the grandeur and dignity of that body, that its powers and prerogatives should be shared by an influx of unknown and insignificant people from remote and subordinate provinces. The idea of admitting delegates from the settlers in wild woods three thousand miles away, to a share in the government of old England, was wholly inadmissible.

Nor was the plan any more acceptable to the colonists themselves. They knew very well that if the plan were adopted at all it would be only a very small number of representatives that the colonists would be allowed to elect, and that these would sooner or later consist of scheming and ambitious men, who, when they found themselves so far away from their constituents, and entirely removed from any possible supervision, would be easily led by the bribes and blandishments of the government to vote pretty much as the government pleased. The colonists were determined to be satisfied with nothing less than having their own legislative assemblies on their own ground, and to have the revenues of the colonies entirely under the control of those assemblies, just as those of the parent country were under that of the Parliament of England.

The government, on the other hand, were resolved that the Parliament of England, elected by a portion of the people of England alone, should be the supreme legislature of the empire and act as the virtual representative of the whole imperial population.

On this point the colonists and the mother country were to take issue.

CHAPTER III
THE STAMP ACT

THE FIRST ATTEMPTED TAXATION

When the British minister had finally come to the conclusion that the plan of taxing the colonies in America by the home government, and without the consent of the colonial legislatures, should be carried into effect, it became very important to determine in what form the experiment should first be made. There is a great difference in different taxes, in respect to the difficulty of collecting them, and also in respect to the facility with which they can be resisted or evaded. It was finally determined that the first tax should be levied on legal and business documents, and should be collected by stamps. The law which Parliament passed to carry this measure into effect became afterward greatly celebrated in history under the name of the Stamp Act. It provided that all business documents, such as deeds, leases, receipts, drafts, bills of exchange, promissory notes and the like, in order to be of legal validity must have certain stamps attached to them, which stamps were to be purchased beforehand of government officers appointed to sell them. The money thus obtained by the sale of the stamps constituted the tax. There were several important advantages in this plan which admirably adapted it to the end which the government had in view.

ADVANTAGES OF THE PLAN

There were three special advantages which seemed to characterize this particular plan.

1. The tax being collected in the form of money received for the sale of the stamps to stationers and others, who would have to keep supplies for their customers, would be received in advance by the government, in large sums, and so not only would all the expense

and trouble of collecting it of individuals be saved, but all danger of irritating collisions with the people by tax gatherers, and all questions in respect to the amount which each one was to pay would be avoided.

2. The plan seemed to deprive individuals, too, of all opportunity and all means of resisting the tax. No one was absolutely called upon to pay anything. If a man wished to buy a house, he could not have a valid title unless he had a stamp upon the deed, and this stamp he would have to pay for. But this stamp he was not obliged to buy. If he was willing to go without his house, or if he could content himself with a title to it not valid in law, he could do so. Thus, the tax came to him in the form, not of a claim, but of the offer of a privilege. The government did not come to him saying—"Pay us a tax"—but, "If you buy a stamp of us, we will give you a legal title to the house you want to buy. If not, not. You can do just as you please about it."

Putting a man in this position, they thought, would render him entirely helpless in resisting the tax.

The government knew very well that there were many persons in the colonies who were prepared to resist in the most desperate manner, and at all hazards, the attempt to collect money of them under authority of an act of Parliament, and they thought it probable that if it were proposed to collect a tax in any ordinary way they would refuse to pay, and that when the officers should attempt to seize their property, they would call upon the people to assist them, and that serious riots, and perhaps extended insurrections, might ensue. But on this plan, all such opportunities to make disturbance would be avoided, inasmuch as nobody would be directly called upon to pay any money. The most, therefore, that any malcontent could do would be to refuse to use the stamps; but this, it seemed, would only injure himself by interrupting and embarrassing his business. They thought there were enough who would use the stamps in any event, to set the machinery of the system in motion, and that the malcontents, having nothing tangible to resist, would exhaust their hostility in vain threats and angry remonstrances, and then, finding themselves helpless, would gradually, one after another, fall in, and in the end, the country would acquiesce in what it could not help, and all would go well.

3. The third advantage, or rather favorable characteristic of the plan, as it was carried out in the act of Parliament, was, that the prices fixed for the several stamps required were very low. This they thought would make the people much less eager to resist the measure. In fact, the object of the government in this first step, was not to collect any considerable amount of money, but only to establish the principle that Parliament claimed the right to tax the colonies, and that they had power to carry the claim into effect. This principle, once acquiesced in by the colonies on a small scale, might afterward, they thought, be easily extended to any limit required.

GREAT EXCITEMENT IN AMERICA

As soon as the news of the passage of the Stamp Act arrived in America, it produced the greatest excitement. Parties immediately began to be formed, one for and one against the government. Of course, all the officers of state that held their appointments directly or indirectly from the king, took sides in favor of the law. Among these officers were the judges in some of the principal courts. There were also a great number of wealthy merchants, and other aristocratic people in the large cities, who, together with many of the more humble classes that were in various ways dependent upon them, or at least under their influence, also took the same side. The persons thus interested in sustaining the government, though comparatively few in number, were influential from their wealth and position; and they formed quite a formidable party. They soon received the name of Tories—while those who opposed the taxation—constituting, in fact, the great bulk of the population in nearly all the colonies, called themselves Whigs.

PERIOD WHEN THESE TRANSACTIONS OCCURRED

The Stamp Act was passed in the spring of 1765. This was eight or ten years before the actual commencement of hostilities between the colonies and mother country took place. All this long interval was spent in disputes and discussions, growing more and more bitter every year, and in the gradual taking of sides by the various classes of the community, as well as in the making of preparations on the one part and on the other for the final conflict.

The act was passed, as is stated above, in the spring of 1765. The news arrived in America a few weeks later. The system was, however, not to go into effect until the following November. This delay was necessary, in some measure, in order to allow time for the designing and printing of the stamps in England, and for sending over and distributing a sufficient supply to all the colonies, so that they might be ready in the hands of the various officers appointed to sell them, when the time for putting the system into operation should arrive. It was thought, also, that this delay would allow time for the excitement, which it was well known the first tidings of the adoption of the measure would necessarily awaken in the colonies, to subside.

"They will, doubtless, be furious at the outset," said the British ministers to themselves, "when the news first reaches them; but the lapse of a few months will allow them time to cool, and by November, they will find that it is useless for them to resist, and so will quietly submit."

THE EXCITEMENT DOES NOT SUBSIDE

But, as the summer months passed away, the excitement, instead of appearing to subside, went on continually increasing and extending. The discussion was carried on among the people with great vehemence, in pamphlets and newspapers, and also in harangues from orators in public meetings convened to consider the crisis. The legislatures of the different colonies took up the subject, and after very earnest and excited debates, passed resolutions reaffirming the right which they alleged was the common birthright of all Englishmen, to control by their own chosen representatives, the extent and the nature of the taxation which they were called upon to sustain.

THE TRUE POINT AT ISSUE

And here I must remind my readers again that they must not lose sight of the true point at issue in this dispute, which was, not whether the colonies should be taxed for their proper proportion of the expenses of the imperial government, but whether the mode and measure of their taxation should be controlled by their own representatives, or by the representatives of the English people at home. "You," said the colonists, in effect, to the English people, "claim the right through your representatives, to regulate and control all the taxation that is to be imposed upon you. We only claim the same right, in behalf of our representatives, to superintend the taxation that is to be imposed upon us. Just grant to us, in our distant settlements beyond the seas, the same rights and privileges that you yourselves claim at home, and that is all that we require."

On the other hand the government maintained that the Parliament, though the members were elected by voters residing within the kingdom alone, formed the supreme legislature of the empire, and though chosen by a portion only of the king's subjects, virtually represented the whole.

GENERAL CONVENTION CALLED

Besides the resolutions that were passed by the different colonial legislatures, protesting against the obnoxious law, the legislature of Massachusetts took a much more decided step by proposing that a convention should be called of delegates from all the colonies, to meet in New York and consider the crisis, and concert some common action for averting the danger. They passed resolutions to this effect, which when approved by the governor were to be sent to the other colonies, inviting them to appoint delegates to attend the proposed convention.

So much time would however be required for convening the legislatures to elect the delegates, and for the various consultations and discussions to which the project would give rise, and also for the journeys of the delegate; some of whom would have to come from distant provinces by the slow and toilsome modes of traveling in usage in those days, that the period for the meeting of the convention could not be fixed earlier than the second week in October, which was only three weeks before the time that the Stamp Act was to go into effect.

This was in one respect a favorable circumstance, as it made the governor less unwilling to approve the act of the legislature, and without his approval it could not pass. The governor was of course in favor of sustaining the tax, and was consequently interested in thwarting and hindering all plans of the colonists for opposing it. But he seems to have thought that by refusing his assent to the act of the legislature calling the convention, he might only increase the excitement of the people, and so do more injury than the convention itself could do, especially as it was not to meet until so near the time at which the Stamp Act was to go into operation, that the proceedings of the body could have little immediate effect.

Besides, in the resolutions passed by Massachusetts calling the convention, the object was stated to be to prepare a joint remonstrance or protest, on the part of all the colonies, to be forwarded to the king, praying him to withdraw the obnoxious measure. And the governor seems to have thought that if the colonies would be satisfied with banding themselves together only for the purpose of remonstrance and protest, he might as well allow them to have their own way.

This project of a convention seemed to look only to peaceful and legal modes of opposing the tax, but unfortunately any remedy which could be applied by these means seemed too tardy for the impatience of the people, and before the time arrived when the stamps were to be offered for sale, and the law put in force, serious riots, and other very alarming disturbances, broke out in several of the large cities and towns.

PREPARATIONS MADE IN BOSTON FOR COLLECTING THE TAX

The excitement which in the end led to the riots seems to have been increased by the preparations that were made in Boston for collecting the tax. A person named Oliver was appointed by the government to sell the stamps, and he prepared a small building in what is now State Street for the stamp office, where merchants and others were to come and purchase their supplies when the time for opening the sale should arrive. This greatly increased the excitement, and evoked much angry discussion, and many threats, from people assembled at the corners of the streets and in other public places.

The Liberty Tree

The favorite place of assembling, especially for persons belonging to the middling and lower classes of society was under a great tree which stood in the road leading out of the town toward the Neck, not far from where Boylston market now stands. The tree was a large spreading elm, at that time about fifty years old. It stood before a house that was nearly opposite the present market, and for some reason or other it was quite a place of resort during the pleasant summer evenings, and ultimately it became the headquarters of the most violent opposers of the Stamp Act, and received the name of The Liberty Tree.

The Effigies

At length one morning about the middle of August, the attention of the passersby along the road was attracted to two effigies which they saw suspended in the tree, and very soon a great crowd was collected at the spot. One of these effigies represented Mr. Oliver, the stamp officer who was preparing his stamp office in State Street. The other was a monstrous boot, with an image of the devil peeping out at the top of it. This last "pageantry" as the writers of the day called it, was intended to denote Lord *Bute*, an English minister, who had taken a very active part in procuring the enactment of the Stamp Act, and who was consequently the object of special resentment and hostility in America.

Governor Hutchinson

One of the most prominent of the public men at this time on the stage in Massachusetts was Hutchinson, commonly known in history as Governor Hutchinson, though he was not governor at this time. At the period of the Stamp Act he was the chief justice of Massachusetts, an appointment which he held from the British government; and though he was a native of Boston, and had lived nearly all his life in the colony, all his political influence was devoted to the service of the home government, and to supporting the powers and prerogatives of the crown.

It was of course very convenient for the British ministry to have an able and influential colonist on their side in these controversies. So they rewarded Hutchinson generously with offices and honors, and he looked exclusively to the home government for support; while yet in his dealings with the people of the colony he was careful to act always with moderation and discretion, and to manifest a sufficient degree of regard for the opinions and wishes of the people, to preserve his influence among them. He was in a word one of that class of politicians that are strenuous for upholding and preserving the authority of the powers that be, and assiduous in cultivating the favor of the rich and great.

Governor Hutchinson was, however, a very superior man, both in respect to natural ability and literary attainments. He was educated at Harvard College, and afterward studied law in Boston. During the whole course of his life, he took a great deal of interest in everything relating to the history of the colony, and to its growth and prosperity; and he had collected before this time a great number of valuable books and manuscripts relating to the early history of Massachusetts and New England, all which he was preserving with great care, in a handsome residence which he occupied in the town.

Oliver, the officer appointed to furnish the stamps, was the brother-in-law of Governor Hutchinson—or rather of Chief Justice Hutchinson, for that was the title by which he was designated at the period in question.

PLANS FOR REMOVING THE EFFIGIES

As soon as the chief justice was informed of the effigies which had been hung in the night in the great elm tree, he directed the sheriff to go and take them down.

But the sheriff did not do it. All the force which the officer of a court has at his command, consists first of his own deputies, who are very few in number, and then of such other citizens as he may find at hand, and summon to aid him in executing the law. Such a force as this usually proves amply sufficient for arresting single criminals, or attaching property in ordinary civil suits; but in this case the sheriff seems to have been afraid that it would not be sufficient to enable him to take down the effigies from the midst of the large and excited crowd that was gathered around the tree.

The governor of the colony also, Bernard, was very indignant at the outrage, as he considered it, and brought the subject before his council, with a view of causing the effigies to be taken down by means of the military force under his command—for, while a sheriff, in executing the mandate of a judge, has power only to call upon citizens to aid him, the governor of any state or colony, being in command of the military force, can call out a body of troops to enforce his authority, should occasion require.

The council, however, deemed it inexpedient to resort to military force, in this case. They thought it more prudent to leave the effigies on the tree, as any attempt to remove them by the troops would only increase and prolong the excitement, which they supposed, if the government took no notice of the affair, would soon subside.

So the effigies remained on the tree, and were surrounded all the day by crowds of people continually coming and going, and all in a state of great excitement. Some scowled with anger, and uttered dark threats and imprecations. Others pelted the hanging effigies with sticks and stones, and filled the air with derisive laughter, mockings and jeers.

An Open Riot

Thus far there had been no actual breach of the peace or violation of law—nothing but the hanging of effigies upon a tree. During the day, however, a plan was formed among the leaders, for some more decided action. The plan was to take down the effigies that evening, and march with them in procession down King Street, as the present State Street was then called, and demolish the stamp office which Oliver had provided there, and then to proceed to Fort Hill, where Mr. Oliver lived, and there to burn the effigies in a bonfire, to be made for the purpose in the street, in front of Mr. Oliver's house.

This plan was, accordingly, carried into effect. As soon as it was dark, a large crowd collected under the great tree, and the leaders immediately proceeded to take down the effigies, and to convey them, at the head of a rude and noisy throng, along what is now Washington Street to King Street, and there they entirely demolished the stamp office building. This was not a difficult task, as the building was a small one, and built of wood. After accomplishing this work, the tumultuous procession was formed again, and marched, bearing the effigies and attended by a noisy throng of men and boys, to the appointed place at Fort Hill, where they proceeded to the work of making a bonfire.

In the meantime, some of Mr. Oliver's friends—among them the chief justice himself—hearing of the disturbance, repaired to the spot, and began to concert some measures for putting a stop to the proceedings. This, however, only exasperated the rioters, and made them more furious than ever, and they finally attacked Mr. Oliver's house. The family made their escape, and the mob commenced breaking the windows and injuring the furniture. After doing considerable damage of this kind, they went away.

The next day, Mr. Oliver, who seems to have been by this time thoroughly alarmed, authorized his friends to announce that he had resigned his position as stamp officer. The populace were, however, not satisfied with this, but insisted that he should come to the great elm tree, and there publicly declare his renouncement of the office. The tree itself now began to be greatly celebrated. It was about this time that it received its name. The space around it, in the open air, they called Liberty Hall, and here the populace held nightly assemblages, to confer together, and listen to the harangues of orators, denouncing the attempts of the government of Great Britain to govern and tax them through the action of the English Parliament, instead of through their own proper legislatures, and to reiterate their solemn determination never to submit.

All these proceedings, though plainly of a lawless and riotous character, were approved, or at least were not condemned by the better portion of the community. Rioting in theory was wrong, they admitted, as people always do; but then, in this case, all other remedies seemed too tardy in their operation, and the people could not be much blamed for taking the case into their own hand. The blame was not for them, but for the government that had passed the outrageous law which they were resisting. This is the way, in fact, that people generally reason in respect to riots which are aimed at the accomplishment of political ends which they approve.

Besides in this case the mob had thus far really shown some degree of moderation. They had done no serious mischief except to destroy the stamp office, which everybody admitted ought to have been destroyed.

RIOTING AS A REMEDY FOR WRONG

Although the principle of riotous resistance to law is never approved by anyone as a legitimate and safe remedy for the unjust or oppressive measures of government, yet it has generally been found, in times of public excitement, that any party is prone to justify, or at least is found to condemn very faintly, any acts of lawless violence perpetrated on *their* side. This is especially the case at the commencement of the proceedings, which are usually marked with a certain degree of moderation, which however soon entirely disappears.

The truth is that although men actuated only by a sense of honest indignation against an oppressive law may begin the work, a quite different class of persons always very soon come forward to carry it on. There is always in every community a large number of lawless and desperate men, who like nothing better than an opportunity to carry terror and destruction through the streets of a town, and, under pretense of accomplishing some political object, to indulge their own criminal passion for plunder and debauchery. Of course all such men as these, that existed in Boston at this time, joined the party of rioters, and did all they could to increase the excitement and prepare the way for a new and more serious outbreak.

There was no difficulty in doing this, for the more respectable portion of the community seemed to justify what had been done, and this of course encouraged the riotous and desperate men to attempt more. Various circumstances occurred, and many rumors were circulated, which tended to widen and deepen the general hostility to the government, and to direct it more and more strongly against Chief Justice Hutchinson.

THE SACKING OF HUTCHINSON'S RESIDENCE

At length one night a week or two after the first disturbance, a bonfire was built in the street as a signal to call the mob together. A large and noisy assemblage soon convened, and when they were all ready they proceeded in a crowd to the houses of some persons who were most obnoxious to the people, on account of their connection with the Stamp Act.

They attacked and plundered two houses. One was that of a judge, in one of the courts. They destroyed all the judge's papers and also the records and files belonging to the court. Another was the residence of Mr. Hallowell who was connected with the custom-house. They plundered the house, and then breaking into the cellar they found there a large quantity of wines and liquors, and bringing them out they distributed them among the crowd.

After carousing a short time and becoming partially or wholly intoxicated, the mob set off again toward Hutchinson's house. Many of the men were now in a state of drunken frenzy. When they reached the house they burst open the doors, and began at once pillaging it of everything that was possible to appropriate, and destroying what they could not take away. They found a large sum of money which they seized and divided. They broke up the furniture and the mirrors, defaced and spoiled the paintings, and even battered down many of the interior partitions. They seized all the books and papers which the chief justice had been collecting for so many years, and which would have been of incalculable value to future generations, and bringing them out into the street they piled them up upon a large bonfire and burnt them all.

Finally they went away leaving the house a mass of ruins. Of course while this work was going on, and for the greater part of the remainder of the night, the whole town was in a state of great alarm and anxiety, no one knowing what freak an infuriated and drunken mob might next undertake to play.

CHANGE IN PUBLIC OPINION

Of course after this, public sentiment was entirely changed in respect to the wisdom of encouraging a resort to mobs and riots as a remedy for political wrongs. The whole community at once aroused itself to the necessity of arresting such proceedings as these. A large public meeting of citizens was held the next day, and resolutions were passed condemning the rioters and recommending to the municipal authorities to take vigorous measures to prevent a repetition of such outrages.

Large rewards were offered for discovery of the ringleaders, and yet, though some of them were afterward arrested, there was still so large a portion of the community who sympathized with them, and considered their conduct as at least excusable, that none of them were ever punished.

RIOTS IN OTHER PLACES

The example set by the Bostonians of riotous opposition to the Stamp Act was followed in the principal towns of the other colonies. The chief object aimed at by the mob in all these cases was to compel the persons who had been appointed as distributors of the stamps, to resign their places, to prevent others being appointed in their stead, and also to intimidate other persons of distinction, who were inclined to defend or excuse the tax.

In Providence they paraded effigies of such persons through the streets, with halters around their necks, and then burnt the effigies upon great bonfires, made sometimes of the furniture obtained from the sack of the houses of the obnoxious individuals.

In Newport they destroyed two houses in this way. The stamp distributor saved his, however, by coming out and solemnly promising the mob that he would not attempt to execute his office.

In various places in Connecticut, too, they burnt effigies in this way, and compelled the stamp distributors to resign. In New York they printed a copy of the Stamp Act upon a big placard, headed The Folly of England and the Ruin of America, and paraded it about the streets—a great throng accompanying it, and filling the air with groans and shouts of execration.

In Virginia, in addition to other measures taken, the lawyers held a meeting and solemnly pledged themselves not to conduct any business in court, that had stamps attached to the papers. Thus in case any persons should seem disposed to use the stamps for the sake of having their business transacted legally, they could find no attorney or counselor to take charge of it for them.

In Maryland, the appointed stamp distributor, in order to avoid the danger, fled from the town and went to New York, intending to wait there until the storm should blow over. But his townsmen sent a delegation after him, and made such representations to him, that he thought it most prudent to resign the office.

In Philadelphia, the excitement was as great as in the other towns. All the stamp distributors were compelled to resign, and when the ship which was bringing the stamps from England arrived in the river, and was coming up toward the town, all the vessels set their colors at half-mast, and the bells of all the churches tolled a funeral knell.

Total Failure of the Government to Carry the Act into Effect

The time at length arrived—the first of November—when the law was to go into effect. The day was ushered in everywhere with the most gloomy solemnities. At Boston, the bells were tolled, and all the shops and stores were closed, while effigies of various persons considered as authors and abettors of the law, were carried about the street, and then pulled to pieces or burned. At Portsmouth, the bells were tolled, and a general invitation was given to the people to come and attend the funeral of liberty. A coffin adorned with splendid decorations was prepared, and was inscribed conspicuously with the words: Liberty, Aged cxiv Years.

This coffin was borne solemnly through the streets, accompanied by the music of muffled drums, and by the tolling of the bells and the firing of minute guns. It was conveyed thus to a place where a grave had been dug, and the process of interment was commenced, when suddenly the cry arose that signs of life had appeared, that Liberty was not yet entirely dead. So the coffin was drawn up again, the inscription was changed to Liberty Revived, the bells began to ring merry peals, and the people filled the air with shouts of rejoicing and triumph.

In New York, when the stamps arrived, the governor, fearing that the people might seize them, had them all taken to the fort for safekeeping. The people then seized the governor's coach, and putting an effigy of the governor in it, they drew it through the streets to the public gallows. They bung the effigy on the gallows, with the figure of a devil by the side of it, and an imitation of a bill of lading with a stamp attached to it, suspended near. They finally took down the effigies and the gallows, and piling them upon the coach, they proceeded to the governor's house, and there burnt them—coach, gallows, effigies and all, before his eyes.

Such demonstrations as these showed very clearly the popular feeling, but there was a much more decided and substantial proof of the resolute determination of the Americans, never to submit to the law, in the fact that the use of the stamps throughout all the colonies, in all business and legal transactions was persistently and obstinately refused. The consequence was immense difficulty and embarrassment for all concerned. For a time, business was almost entirely suspended, but it was gradually resumed without using the stamps, notwithstanding the illegality of all papers not thus authenticated.

In addition to this, the people in many of the principal towns, by way of retaliation upon the people of England for attempting, through their Parliament to usurp an unjust authority over them, held public meetings and resolved to abstain from the use of all English manufactures. They resolved to make everything they possibly could for themselves, and what they could not thus contrive to manufacture in some way or other, they would do without. They would spin their own wool into yarn, and weave cloth from it at home, and in order that the supply of wool might not fail, they resolved to buy no more mutton or lamb in the market, in order that the animals might all be saved for their wool.

These resolutions, and the measures taken in furtherance of them, were carried into effect to such an extent, that the trade of the English merchants with the colonies was very much curtailed, and the merchants began to find great fault with the government for having pursued a policy tending thus to exasperate and drive away from them their best customers.

REPEAL OF THE STAMP ACT

The passage of the Stamp Act through Parliament was by no means unanimous. There was a large party in England that were strongly opposed to it, and they resisted it most strenuously at the time it was enacted; some on the ground that the Americans were right, and that the Parliament chosen in England to represent the people of England, had no power to assess taxes or legislate in any way for a different and distant community in America. Others condemned the measure as impolitic, and as only tending to create difficulty and disturbance in America, to no useful end.

These persons were, however, outvoted, and the law was passed, but now that the difficulties and disturbances which they had predicted had really occurred, so as to verify in full, and more than verify, their predictions, their influence in the councils of the nation greatly increased. They began to call for a repeal of the law. The merchants, too, who found that they were suffering from the loss of their trade, began to remonstrate. These and other difficulties occurring in England led to changes in the ministry which facilitated a change of policy.

It was finally decided to repeal the law, but in order to soothe their wounded pride, and to soften the mortification of being obliged to retreat from the position they had taken, the ministers first carried through Parliament what they called a declaratory act, solemnly affirming that the king and Parliament *had the right* to make laws "to bind the colonies and people of America, subjects of the British crown, in *all cases whatsoever.*"

This declaration having been made, the bill for the repeal of the Stamp Act was brought in. It was prefaced by a preamble, which assigned as a reason for the repeal, that "the continuance of the act would be attended with many inconveniences, and might be productive of serious detriment to the commercial interests of the kingdom."

The original friends of the bill would, however, not give up the point without a very earnest and protracted struggle. They resisted to the last, and the debate which took place on the question of repeal was one of the most excited and violent discussions which ever occurred in the British Parliament. A great many petitions and remonstrances were read, some for and some against the repeal. Many of these were from merchants and mercantile bodies in London. Others were from the different legislatures in America. A petition was presented from the convention of delegates from the colonies which had been held in New York, but it was not received, on the ground that the convention was a body not known to the British constitution.

The debate continued all night. At length, at three o'clock in the morning, the vote was taken in the House of Commons. There were two hundred and seventy-five in favor of, and one hundred and sixty-seven against the repeal. The bill was immediately carried to the House of Lords by the mover, attended by about two hundred of the other members.

There followed another debate in the House of Lords, but the bill finally passed that body, and in due time received the signature of the king—and the Stamp Act was at an end.

SATISFACTION AND JOY OF THE AMERICANS

The news of the repeal of the Stamp Act was received everywhere in America with the most joyful acclamations. The bells were rung, bonfires and illuminations were kindled, processions were formed, and votes of thanks to Parliament and to the king were passed by the various colonial assemblies. All with one accord determined to resume at once the usual commercial intercourse with England, and the purchase and use of English manufactures. At a great public meeting in Philadelphia, it was unanimously resolved, "That to demonstrate our zeal to Great Britain, and our gratitude for the repeal of the Stamp Act, each of us will, on the fourth of June next, being the birthday of our gracious sovereign, dress ourselves in a new suit of the manufactures of Great Britain, and give what homespun clothes we have to the poor."

CHAPTER IV
PROGRESS OF THE QUARREL

The Controversy not Settled by the Repeal of the Stamp Act

The repeal of the Stamp Act operated to suspend only, the great controversy between the colonies and the mother country, and not at all to bring it to a close. It settled nothing, for by the declaratory act which accompanied it, and by which the right of Parliament to legislate for the colonies was affirmed in the most formal manner, and in the most absolute terms, it was made plain that Parliament and the government only retreated from the position they had taken for the purpose of gaining ground for a new and more decided advance, in some other direction.

Thus, although the mass of the population received the news of the repeal with unbounded exultation, the joy of the more thoughtful and farseeing men was mingled with a great many gloomy forebodings. Indeed, many of the more prominent statesmen began to prepare their minds for the renewal of the conflict, which they thought would not probably be very long deferred. They even began to concert measures for putting the country in a state of readiness to meet the emergency, when it should arrive.

Unfavorable Turn of Affairs in England

It was not long before things seemed to take a more unfavorable turn in England, in respect to America. The friends of the colonies who had succeeded in securing and retaining a controlling influence long enough to effect the repeal of the act, soon began to lose ground again. There were changes in the ministry which brought men of the other party into power. When the danger, too, resulting from the disturbances in the colonies, and the interruption to the commerce of the London merchants had passed away, a great many persons, who had been aroused to action while the crisis continued, retired again, now that it was past, and left the field to the others, who thus soon found their party strong enough to begin to plan new measures for bringing the refractory colonies to a proper state of subjection to the government at home.

Dispute about the Damages

One of the first questions which led to a renewal of the ill feeling, was the question about the damages to be paid for the mischief done by the rioters. Hutchinson and the others whose houses and property had been destroyed petitioned the home government to require the colonists to make good their losses. In consequence of this, the minister in charge of the colonial affairs wrote a circular letter to all the governors of the colonies, in which, after expatiating in very imposing language upon "the lenity, the moderation and the forbearance," which Parliament had displayed toward the colonies in all its late dealings with them, and the obligations the colonists were under to show "their respectful gratitude and cheerful obedience in return for such a signal display of indulgence and affection," directed that by order of Parliament all those persons who had been injured in any way, by the populace, in consequence of their agency in respect to the Stamp Act, should be fully compensated by the several colonies in which the disturbances had occurred.

Of course, the several governors transmitted this circular to the legislatures of their respective colonies. Governor Bernard, of Massachusetts, accompanied it with a very urgent call to the assembly to make an immediate grant for this purpose.

The assembly resented so keenly the haughty and dictatorial tone which the governor assumed in this communication, that they voted at first that they would not make any grant, but would endeavor to ascertain who the persons were that had committed the mischief, and compel *them* to pay the damage. This led to another angry communication from the governor, and at length, after a good deal of delay, and many sharp communications between the parties, the assembly finally voted to make compensation for the damage, but at the same time they passed a bill of complete indemnity for all who had been concerned in the riots. They seemed to consider it just that if a government failed to protect its subjects or citizens from lawless violence, they ought to make good the loss—but that if they did so, they had a right to shield the men who caused it, under the impulse of an honest though mistaken patriotism, from being molested for the offence. They were not willing to gratify the losers by allowing them the double atonement of recovering from the community the amount of the damage done, and punishing the actors for doing it.

RENEWED ATTEMPT TO TAX THE COLONISTS

The British government waited about a year before renewing the attempt to tax the colonists. They seemed to have hoped that by the lapse of a little time the excitement would subside. But it did not subside. The colonists were vigilant, and felt the necessity of being on their guard. They kept up a recollection of the Stamp Act quarrel by speeches, writings in the newspapers, and celebrations of various kinds, by means of which, they not only commemorated the triumph they had already achieved, but also kept the spirit of resistance alive in the minds of the people, and made them always ready for a new contest, whenever the occasion should arise.

The occasion was not long deferred. In a little more than a year from the time that the Stamp Act was repealed, a law was passed in Parliament laying an external or customs tax, upon five articles which it was supposed were so essential to the wants of the colonists, that the people could not possibly dispense with the use of them, and were, at the same time, so exclusively of foreign production, that they could not furnish them, nor obtain substitutes for them at home.

These five articles were *glass, lead, paints, paper* and *tea.* The act taxing these articles was passed in May, 1767. The Stamp Act had been repealed in the spring of the preceding year.

THE IDEA OF THE GOVERNMENT

The Stamp Act, as has been already explained, was of the nature of a *direct* or *internal* tax—that is, it was a tax levied *within the country*

47

on the property or business of the people. In that respect the measure was entirely new, the government having never before attempted any internal taxation in any of the colonies. They had required duties of various kinds to be paid on goods imported, and custom-houses had been established, and custom-house officers appointed, in all the ports, for the collection of the dues. The colonists were accustomed to this, and had made no strenuous objection to it, chiefly because thus far the duties which had been laid on the different kinds of merchandise imported had been intended for the purpose chiefly of regulating the commerce of the colonists, and not for raising a revenue from them. But, by the act now passed, the duties laid were high enough to afford an appreciable amount for revenue, and yet not high enough, as the government supposed, to awaken any very decided opposition. The idea of the government was, that as they had given up the attempt to carry out the scheme of direct taxation, and as the present law only established an assessment on foreign merchandise imported into the country—a department of legislation which it had been generally admitted in the colonies came fairly within the jurisdiction of Parliament—there would be no violent opposition to the proposed plan—especially as the articles in question were objects of prime necessity in all new countries, and were, moreover of such a character, that neither the commodities themselves, nor any substitutes for them could possibly be produced in America.

Preparations for a Contest

The state of public feeling, however, in America was such, and such was the tone and spirit manifested by the different legislatures in the proceedings which took place in them from time to time, and in the writings and speeches of private individuals, that the government thought it best to be prepared. So they sent out some fresh bodies of troops; they appointed a special board of commissioners to superintend the custom-house arrangements, and took other precautions of a similar nature, which they thought must operate to intimidate the colonists, and at any rate would greatly strengthen the hands of the government in a contest, in case any contest should arise.

EFFECT OF THESE MEASURES IN AMERICA

The various measures adopted by the English government to prepare for a new contest with the colonies, instead of intimidating and discouraging the Americans, only had the effect of exciting them to a greater spirit of resistance, and to the work of making counter preparations, in order that they themselves might be prepared for the conflict when the time should come. They discussed the questions at issue in the legislatures and in public meetings, and they resisted, step by step, all the efforts made by the English government to strengthen its foothold among them. They made difficulty about providing accommodations for the soldiers sent out. They remonstrated against the new arrangements made for collecting customs, and when, at length, they found that the tax on the five articles of merchandise was really to be laid, they held public meetings, and resolved again to discontinue, as far as possible, all use of British manufactures of every kind. The colony of Massachusetts seems to have taken the lead in these movements, and among the individual men who were most prominent and most powerful in their influence over their countrymen, in respect to the political action of the colonies at this time, were the two patriots whose names became subsequently so celebrated—John Hancock and Samuel Adams.

JOHN HANCOCK

John Hancock was a young merchant of Boston, being at this time but little more than thirty years old. His father died when he was quite young and he was adopted, as it were, by his uncle, a very wealthy merchant of Boston, who sent him to Harvard College to receive his education, and then took him into business with him. In a few years his uncle died, and left him in possession of a very extensive business and of a very large fortune. All this happened about the time of the commencement of the difficulties between England and the colonies, and in 1767, the time at which the act levying duties on the five articles of merchandise was passed, he was living, in the height of his prosperity, in Boston, and carrying on a very extensive business. His rank and social position in the town were very elevated, and his talents and accomplishments, and other excellent personal qualities, greatly increased the influence which his wealth and position commanded. He occupied, moreover, a very elegant mansion on a hill just out of the town, where he lived magnificently, and in the exercise of a liberal hospitality. He had a great taste for sumptuous entertainments, and for other expensive pleasures. He was, moreover, a very open-hearted and generous man, giving largely to public charities and to other objects of general interest to the community. In a word, he was a talented, accomplished, elegant and very popular young man, with all the advantages and means of influence which wealth and the most extended business and social connections could give, entirely at his command. If anyone by his position in society could have been expected to be a conservative, that is, a supporter of the privileges and immunities of existing power, we might have expected that John Hancock would be the man.

SAMUEL ADAMS

Adams was a man of a very different stamp from this. He was considerably older than Hancock, being at this time about forty-five, and by constitutional temperament he was calm, quiet, sedate, and sometimes austere. He exhibited a degree of sternness and severity of character which was far less attractive in the estimation of mankind than the ardent, impulsive and generous character of Hancock. He was not rich, and he lived in a very plain and simple manner, which contrasted strongly with Hancock's profuse expenditure. If he had been possessed of wealth, it might, perhaps, have made no difference with him in this respect, for he was very strict and rigid in all his ideas of right and wrong, and everything like self-indulgence and gaiety was entirely foreign to his nature.

He was educated at Harvard College, and had early gone into public life. He had been elected a member of the general assembly a few years before this time, and had at once begun to distinguish himself by his knowledge of public affairs, and by the extraordinary capacity he manifested in the management of them. He soon acquired a great ascendancy in the legislature, was elected to the office of clerk, and placed upon all important committees; and during the period of the excitement in respect to the Stamp Act, he had exercised great influence in shaping the public policy of the colony, and in the adoption of all the measures aimed at thwarting or resisting the encroachment of the government. In a word, he was at the head of the organized political resistance to the English policy, as Hancock was of that which was manifested in mercantile and business circles, and in social life.

Some time after this period, when the English leaders found out how much the persistence and vigor of the opposition to their measures in America were due to Samuel Adams, they wrote out to Hutchinson, who was then governor of the colony, to inquire why they did not pacify the man by giving him some lucrative office, under the king—which, it seems, had been the usual way of silencing turbulent malcontents in England. Hutchinson, in reply, said that "Such is the obstinacy and inflexible disposition of the man, that he can never be conciliated by any office or gift whatever."

The names of these two men, strikingly dissimilar as they were in character, and in the species of influence they wielded, became afterward inseparably associated with each other in history, from the fact, that some years later, after the revolution had been fully inaugurated, the British government made these two the only exceptions to an offer of pardon which they tendered to the colonists on condition of their returning to their allegiance. Thus, the government, by setting them apart as the only two rebels whose offenses were absolutely unpardonable, placed them on a grand pedestal in the eyes of all coming generations, as the two noblest patriots of the day.

JOHN HANCOCK'S SLOOP *LIBERTY*

The conflict between the colonies and the mother country went on, in a teasing, irritating and resultless manner, as already described, until at length, in the summer of 1768, an incident occurred in relation to one of John Hancock's vessels which greatly increased the popular excitement in Boston though, in this case, it would seem that the colony, or rather the population acting in its behalf, was the party most to be blamed.

51

Landing of John Hancock's wine.

It seems that the commissioners of customs, who had been sent out from England to superintend the arrangements of the custom-houses, made new and more stringent rules in respect to the examination of cargoes, and to the exacting in full, and without any abatement, the amount of the duty required. Certain relaxations of the strict letter of the law had always been customary at the colonial ports, so that at length the enjoyment of them had come to be considered by the merchants as a matter of right. The new commissioners, however, in their zeal to bring the colonies into complete subjection, were disposed to put an end to all indulgences, and they refused to make these allowances anymore. These led to many remonstrances and complaints, but the first time that any real difficulty resulted, was in the case of a vessel belonging to Hancock—the sloop *Liberty*—which arrived in Boston about this time with a quantity of Madeira wine on board.

The deputy custom-house officer—Thomas Kirk—who came on board to collect the dues, refused to make the customary allowance. Whereupon the captain, with the assistance of the crew, took him down into the cabin and locked him up there, and then proceeded, during the night, to put all the wine on shore and store it in the warehouse.

After the wine was all safe on shore, the imprisoned officer was set at liberty.

The next morning, the captain of the sloop proceeded to the custom-house and entered there, in regular form, such a portion of the cargo as he deemed, according to established usage, to be fairly subject to duty. The collector immediately sent down and seized the sloop for a false entry. As fast as news of these proceedings spread about the town, they produced great excitement. Crowds of people collected about the wharf, and the custom-house officers began to fear that they were intending to rescue the sloop from the government authorities by violence. So they cast her off from the wharf, and took her out under the guns of a man-of-war—the *Romney*—which was lying in the harbor, ready for any emergency of this kind that might occur.

The sight of the sloop lying thus near the *Romney*, with the guns of the latter pointing toward the town in token of defiance, greatly increased the excitement. The crowds in the street increased, and soon became an angry and uncontrollable mob. They proceeded to the houses of the principal officers of the customs, where they broke the windows, and committed such other acts of violence that the officers fled for their lives. The officers made their escape first to the *Romney,* and then to Castle William, which was a strong fortress built on one of the islands of the harbor, and garrisoned by English troops. The mob, finding that the men had escaped them, took possession of the collector's boat, and after dragging it through the streets in triumph for some time, they finally made a bonfire of it on the common.

The authorities of the town afterward disavowed and condemned these proceedings, though they claimed that the people were in some sense excusable for their violence on account of the great provocation which the English custom-house officers had given them, by taking away the vessel of one of their leading merchants, and placing her under the guns of a man-of-war in so insulting a manner. They, however, did not justify the riot, and they offered a reward for the detection of the ring-leaders, in order that they might be punished. But, though everybody knew who they were, there was no one found who would inform against them, and so they were never molested.

THE CIRCULAR LETTER OF MASSACHUSETTS

Besides these conflicts between the people and the authorities, which were continually breaking out in all the large cities in America during the progress of the quarrel, there occurred, from time to time, more serious, though less violent altercations, between the English government at home and the various legislative assemblies of the colonies. A good example of these official and legislative skirmishings is afforded by the proceedings which took place in relation to what is called in history the Massachusetts circular.

OCCASION OF THE CIRCULAR

The reader will, perhaps, recollect that in the time of the Stamp Act, the assembly of Massachusetts issued a call for a convention of delegates chosen by the various colonies to be held in New York, and that this convention was held, and that it passed some important resolutions. This proceeding gave great offence to the English government. A government is always especially alarmed at anything that looks like a combination among those subject to its sway, and the attempt of the colonies to band themselves together in any way, for the purpose of strengthening themselves in their resistance to any measures of the home government; they considered as little better than open treason.

Accordingly, not to give any unnecessary offence to the home government, the General Assembly of Massachusetts concluded, on the next occasion, which was that of the taxing of the five articles of merchandise as already related, that they would not call a formal convention, but seek the cooperation of the different colonies by means of correspondence, and of concerted though independent action. They accordingly prepared the famous circular, and addressed it to all the colonies.

This circular was expressed in very moderate and cautious language, but it called the attention of the other legislatures very distinctly and decidedly to the persistent attempts of the British ministry and Parliament to tax the colonies without their consent, and proposed to them to take such measures as they might think— each colony for itself—best suited to arrest the evil; and in addition to that, they proposed that the several colonies should join in a remonstrance and petition to the king, being assured, they said, "that the united and dutiful supplications of his distressed American subjects would meet with his royal and favorable acceptance."

It was, however, unfortunately, just the circumstance that these supplications were *united* that tended most decidedly to *prevent* their meeting with his majesty's royal and favorable acceptance.

THE QUESTION OF INDEPENDENCE

The circular was accompanied with forms of a petition which the Massachusetts colony proposed to send to the king, and other similar documents, in which it is noticeable that the Assembly took care specially to deny that they were actuated by any sentiment of disloyalty to their sovereign, or by any desire to make the colonies independent of the mother country, as their enemies had sometimes alleged. They fully acknowledged the supreme authority of the king over all portions of the empire; all that they claimed was, that in exercising this authority over the colonies, he should allow his subjects in America the full enjoyment of the rights and privileges which are secured by the British constitution to every subject of the realm.

It is probable that at this time there was no distinctly formed design of sundering the connection between the colonies and the mother country, but the allusion to such a design in the circular, or in the papers accompanying it, shows that the possibility that such might be the result, was entertained even at this early period—nearly eight years before the Declaration of Independence was finally made.

Displeasure of the Ministry with the Circular

The English ministry were greatly displeased with the legislature of Massachusetts for issuing this circular. A period of two or three months was required in those days for a voyage across the Atlantic and the return, and very soon after the expiration of that time, a communication came to the governor of Massachusetts from the English minister denouncing the action of the assembly in the strongest terms. He was sure, he said, that such a proceeding could not be the free and deliberate act of the assembly. The vote must have been obtained by surprise, or by other improper means, and he directed the governor to make known immediately to the assembly the strong feeling of displeasure with which "that rash and hasty transaction" was regarded by the government at home, and requiring them immediately to rescind it.

At the same time the minister sent communications to all the other colonies, saying that the measure proposed by the Massachusetts assembly was regarded by his majesty as of the most dangerous and factious tendency, calculated to inflame the minds of his good subjects in the colonies, and promote an unwarrantable combination, and to exhibit an open opposition to, and denial of, the authority of the Parliament, and to subvert the true principles of the constitution.

The message of the governor calling upon the assembly of Massachusetts to rescind the action connected with the circular letter, was laid before them in the midst of the excitement produced by the seizure of Hancock's vessel. This was, however, a new assembly, inasmuch as the former one, that is, the one of the preceding winter which had adopted the measure in question, had expired, and a new one had been elected. This new assembly was now required by the message to rescind what had been done, on penalty of dissolution.

The governor had power at any time to dissolve an assembly, if he considered it contumacious or unmanageable, in which case the members of course lost their places, and the country was called upon to proceed to a new election. The dissolution of a legislative body involves thus for all the members of it the loss of their places, and sends them, every one, back to private life, and to new elections, in which all the influence of the government will always be employed in preventing them from being chosen again. Thus the threat on the part of the governor to dissolve the assembly was virtually a threat to punish the members, individually, if they refused to comply with his demands.

DECISION OF THE ASSEMBLY OF MASSACHUSETTS ON THE QUESTION OF RESCINDING

Notwithstanding this threat, the assembly most promptly and decidedly refused to rescind anything. Some of the speakers assumed quite a tone of defiance against the government at home. One of them, James Otis, said in his speech, that instead of calling upon Massachusetts to rescind her measures, the minister would do better to call upon Parliament to rescind theirs—for if Great Britain, he declared, did not soon abandon her attempts to assume unlawful authority and control over the colonies, she would soon find them lost to her forever.

Several of the members, moreover, who had voted against the circular letter, at the time of its passage, now voted against rescinding it, declaring that they would not submit even to royal dictation, in the discharge of their legislative functions.

ADDRESS TO THE MINISTRY ACCOMPANYING THE REFUSAL TO RESCIND

The assembly, moreover, adopted an address to be sent to the ministry, accompanying their refusal to rescind, in which address they stated that the measure of the circular letter, instead of having been hurried through the assembly, or obtained by surprise, was adopted in the middle of the session, and in the most deliberate manner, after full discussion; that it was, moreover, the act of a former assembly, which had fulfilled its functions and ceased to exist. It was now quite incomprehensible to them, they said, how the ministry could call upon them to rescind it, since it was an act that did not relate to something yet to be done, and the farther progress of which might be arrested, but to a measure already fully executed, and carried into complete effect.

"If, however," the letter added, "we are to understand by rescinding, the minister meant passing a vote in disavowal and disapproval of the act, as 'illegal, inflammatory and tending to excite unjustifiable combinations against his majesty's peace, crown and dignity,' then we must take the liberty to testify and publicly to declare, that we hold it to be the native, inherent and indefeasible right of the subjects, *jointly* or severally, to petition the king for a redress of grievances, provided that the same be done in a decent, dutiful, loyal and constitutional way, without tumult, disorder and confusion. If the votes of this house are to be controlled by a minister, we have left to us but a vain semblance of liberty. We have now only to inform you, that this house have voted not to rescind, and that on a division on the question, there were ninety-two nays and seventeen yeas."

Language like this from representatives of the people to a British governor, the direct depository and embodiment of royal prerogative and power, was something wholly unheard of and unknown in British history. There had been, it is true, various discussions and disputes previous to this time, between the king and his humble commons, as the representatives of the people in Parliament usually styled themselves; but in all these controversies the subjects had always assumed a very submissive and supplicating tone, and always seemed to approach the power of the crown in the attitude rather of petitioners begging for forbearance and grace, than of men claiming their rights, and prepared to meet in a hostile and defiant spirit all threatened encroachments upon them.

I refer here only to the tone and language which the commons had been accustomed to use in their contests with the crown, for in respect to measures, they often acted in a very resolute and vigorous manner.

PUBLIC OPINION IN BOSTON ON THE QUESTION OF RESCINDING

The Massachusetts assembly, in order to make their refusal to rescind the more open and defiant, ordered lists of the voters to be printed and circulated through the town. This was also in order, as they said, that the people might know their friends. The list of the nays was received everywhere with applause and demonstrations of honor, while the names of the yeas, that is, of those who voted to rescind, were written out on a great placard, and paraded through the streets with outcries and hootings, and other tokens of contempt and derision. These voters were designated for a long time afterward as the seventeen rescinders.

The governor immediately dissolved the assembly. The people in all the principal towns then held public meetings, and passed resolutions denouncing the governor as a traitor and an enemy of his country.

CHAPTER V
MILITARY PREPARATIONS

EFFECT OF THE DISSOLUTION OF THE ASSEMBLY

Of course, the members of the assembly, when the governor's proclamation dissolving the body was communicated to them, became at once so many private individuals, and for them to have attempted to go on with the transaction of public business would have been open rebellion, and would have legally subjected every one of them so acting to all the pains and penalties of treason. There was nothing for the assembly to do, but to acquiesce in the dissolution and retire to their homes in the various towns and villages of the colony. They carried with them, however, their report of what had been done, and spread everywhere among their constituents the eager spirit of resistance to the measures of the ministry which had been awakened among themselves by their debates, and by the exciting occurrences in which they had taken a part.

Nearly a year would elapse before the governor would be obliged, according to the charter of the colony, to issue the call for a new assembly. It was understood that he had declared that he would not call a new assembly before that time. Consequently, if things were allowed to take their usual course, the colony would be, during all that time, without any means of general or concerted action.

A CONVENTION CALLED

Under these circumstances, the people of Boston conceived the idea of calling a convention, though they must have known very well that such a measure would have greatly increased the anger and exasperation of the royal government. Possibly this very circumstance may have been considered by many of them an additional reason in favor of the measure.

The immediate occasion of the calling of this convention was as follows. The whole military force in the colonies at this time was under the command of General Gage, who afterward took a very prominent part in the events connected with the revolution. General Gage's headquarters were at New York, and not long after the dissolution of the assembly, he sent one of his aids to Boston, to inform the authorities of the town that he expected soon an additional body of troops to arrive there, and to call upon the town to provide quarters for them.

The selectmen,[1] not feeling disposed to take the responsibility of deciding such a question as this, called a town meeting, and the meeting voted promptly that they would not provide quarters for the troops. There was room enough for them, they alleged, in the castle, which, as has already been mentioned, was a strong fortress built on one of the islands in the harbor, and it was there that they properly belonged. They, moreover, sent a message to the governor, requesting him to issue orders for the election of a new assembly in place of the one he had dissolved. The governor refused to do it. The meeting then decided to send out a circular to all the other towns and villages in the colony, proposing to the people to send delegates to a *convention,* to be assembled in Boston for the purpose of consulting on the alarming condition of public affairs, and considering what was to be done.

The plan thus proposed was carried into effect. In due time the delegates were chosen, and in the month of September the convention assembled. This looked very much like a first step on the part of the people toward establishing in some sense a government of their own, independent of the king, and in contravention of the charter of the colony; for the charter expressly provided the mode in which the legislative body should be constituted, and made its duration depend upon the will of the body. The governor, therefore, and the ministry in England, as soon as news arrived there of these proceedings, declared that the calling of the convention was a treasonable act. The colonists replied that the convention which they had called was not intended to exercise any legislative functions at all. They did not claim, nor

---

[1] It has always been the usage in the towns of New England to commit the executive business of the town to a board of three men, chosen annually for this purpose, and called the selectmen.

would they attempt to exercise, any political power whatever. It was only a meeting, they said, of private persons, chosen by direction of the municipal authorities of the towns, it was true, but still only an assembly of private persons, who, having the confidence of their fellow-citizens, met to consult together and consider what was best to be done. There certainly could be no treason in that.

ACTION OF THE CONVENTION

The convention acted strictly in accordance with this view. They did not claim to be a legislative body in any sense, nor attempt to do anything but to pass resolutions and offer petitions. In the resolutions they declared that they were loyal and faithful subjects of the king, that they did not intend any factious opposition to his government, that they were opposed to all riots, and to popular tumults and disorders of every kind. They would do all in their power to suppress every attempt to resist the law by violent means, and they, moreover, strongly recommended patience and good order to their countrymen. All they wished was to adopt peaceable means for preserving for themselves and their descendants, the secure enjoyment of those indefeasible rights which the British constitution vested in every subject of the crown.

They also drew up two petitions. One was addressed to the governor of the colony, and the other to the king.

REJECTION OF THE TWO PETITIONS

The governor at once refused to receive the petition when it was presented to him. He would not recognize the convention, he said, in any way, nor acknowledge it as a legitimate assemblage, but sent back by the messengers his advice to the members composing it, that they should desist from the dangerous and criminal course that they were pursuing. The convention paid no attention to this advice, but proceeded to finish their business of preparing also a memorial to be presented to the king, and then adjourned.

When the memorial of the convention which was intended for the king reached England, the ministers, in the same manner, refused to receive it or to present it to his majesty. They brought the subject up in Parliament, however, and the House of Lords at once passed resolutions condemning the conduct of the people of Massachusetts in the strongest manner, and declaring that the election of deputies to a popular convention, and the assembling of such a convention, were daring insults offered to his majesty's authority, and audacious usurpations of the powers of government, for which it was requisite that the principal actors should be brought to condign and exemplary punishment.

When these resolutions were brought into the House of Commons, they were vehemently resisted there, by some very able men who defended the conduct of the Americans, and condemned in the strongest terms the course which the mother country was pursuing in respect to them. Still they were passed, a large majority being in their favor, and an address was sent to the king approving fully the course which his majesty's government had thus far pursued in respect to the colonies, and praying him to cause the principal leaders in the late treasonable transactions which had taken place in Massachusetts to be arrested and conveyed to England, in order to be there brought to trial.

ARRIVAL OF TROOPS

A few days after the convention adjourned, the political excitement which prevailed in the town of Boston was vastly increased by the appearance of a fleet of six or seven armed vessels in the harbor, with two regiments of British troops on board. This force had been sent to Boston from Halifax, in answer to urgent calls which it afterward appeared had been made by Bernard, the governor of the province, and other persons in high office there, who, in their communication to the ministry in England, had represented to them that the boldness and turbulence of the popular leaders was increasing every day, and that it was absolutely necessary to send there a strong military force to overawe this rising spirit of sedition. The ministers had accordingly sent orders that such a force should be dispatched from Halifax, and it now arrived.

LANDING OF THE TROOPS

The vessels sailed up the harbor till they came near the town, and there deliberately took positions to command it with their guns. After other preparations had been made, the troops were landed—some of the vessels having been first placed in such positions that their guns commanded the landing place, and everything was made ready for firing upon any persons who might assemble there and attempt to prevent the troops from coming on shore.

The force consisted of about seven hundred men. They were to be brought from the vessels in boats to the landing stairs at the end of Long Wharf, a wooden pier extending out to a great distance from the land toward deep water. A truck was placed across the wharf, at some distance from the end, to keep off the crowd, with sentinels placed there to guard the passage.

The troops, in coming to the shore, brought with them a train of artillery, consisting of two field pieces. The men had their guns loaded and their bayonets fixed, and as fast as they reached the shore they were formed in array, as if they were landing in the country of an enemy. Then with drums beating and colors flying, they were marched through the streets to the great common, in what was at that time the outskirts of the town, and there encamped.

QUESTION OF QUARTERS

The governor now sent a communication to the selectmen of the town, informing them that a body of his troops had arrived, and directed them to provide suitable quarters for their accommodation. The selectmen refused to do so. There was the castle, which was in the hands of the military authorities, they said, and entirely at their disposal, and there was ample room in it for the accommodation of the troops. The law was, moreover, that no troops were to be quartered in the town until after all the available space in the forts was filled. To this the governor replied that the quarters remaining unoccupied in the castle were reserved for some other troops which were expected, having been already engaged for them, and so must be considered as filled. The town was, therefore, legally bound to provide accommodations for those that had now arrived. The selectmen, however, still refused to make any provisions for the soldiers.

VIEWS OF THE GOVERNOR

The reason why the governor was not willing to send the troops to the castle, was not because the quarters there were previously engaged, but because he wished to make an imposing military display in the streets of the town, and to have the troops there close at hand, in order to intimidate and overawe the inhabitants. Indeed, it is supposed that the government sought a collision with the people thinking that if they could provoke them to anything like open resistance to their authority, they could at once raise the cry of rebellion and treason, and proceed to take most vigorous military measures for reducing the province to submission, which, so long as the people confined themselves to lawful and peaceable means of resistance, they were in some measure precluded from doing. For if the authorities in America were to proceed in any aggressive manner, against the colonies and without the excuse of any open and violent resistance to the laws, then the party in England which was inclined to defend the cause of the Americans would be greatly increased and strengthened, and the ministry might be overthrown. It was extremely important, therefore, so to manage the affair, as that the contest, if a contest was to come, should be brought on by some act of the people or authorities of the town, which should seem to justify the vigorous measures which the governor was eager to adopt, but which he did not dare to adopt without some plausible excuse. He was very willing, however, it is said by an ostentatious parade of his military force; and by haughty and peremptory demands upon the authorities and people of the town, to give them provocation.

He would, however, probably not have been willing to admit, even to himself, that he wished to incite the people to resistance, but only considered that he had borne with their mutinous and rebellious spirit long enough, and now that he was at length provided with a force sufficient to reduce them to submission, he wished to let them see that he was in earnest, and that they were in his power; and that if they had really entertained any disposition to resist him, he was perfectly willing that they should make the attempt.

So he would not send the troops to the castle, but landing them under the protection of the guns of the ships, and marching them through the town to the common he encamped them there, and then proceeded to demand of the town that they should provide proper quarters for them, as has already been related.

THE MANUFACTORY HOUSE

This demand on the part of the governor that the town should provide quarters for the troops, and the refusal of the authorities to do so, led to various negotiations, in the course of which many curious incidents occurred. It happened that there was at that time in Boston a large building which, for some reason or other, went by the name of the Manufactory House. The building had been let out in apartments to persons of humble station in life, and was now occupied by them; but, as it belonged to the province, and not to any private individual, the governor claimed that it might be assigned to the use of the troops, and one of the regiments was marched to it, and drawn up before it, and the tenants were ordered to withdraw. Of course, a great crowd of spectators had assembled, and among them were some of the principal inhabitants of the town, and they advised the people in the house not to go, but to wait until they were forcibly dispossessed. So the families remained, and the military officers, unwilling to take the first step in the resort to violence, after remaining for some time near the spot, marched the men away.

A COMPROMISE

Finally, however, before night closed in, the difficulty was in a measure compromised, by the consent which was given on the part of the authorities that Faneuil Hall, a large public hall, which has since acquired great celebrity, on account of the important public meetings which have been held in it from time to time, might be occupied by one of the regiments, which, as it happened, was not provided with camp equipage, and that the other should pitch their tents on the Common.

Faneuil Hall proved to be not sufficient for the whole number that were not provided with tents, and so the governor took it upon himself to open the town-house to them, on the ground that the town-house, being also used for the meetings of the general assembly, might be considered as pertaining to the province in some sense, and so under his control as governor.

This town-house was the old building standing at the head of what is now State Street, but which was then called King Street. It seems that the upper stories contained the rooms occupied by the assembly, the lower part forming an open hall, which was used by the merchants as an exchange. The whole building was given up to the use of the soldiers except one room, which had been appropriated to the governor himself for the meetings of his council, and this was reserved.

GREAT EXCITEMENT ON THE FOLLOWING DAY

It was on Saturday—October 1, 1768—that the troops were landed. The various negotiations and arrangements described in the last paragraph, occupied all Saturday night and the greater part of Sunday. During Sunday the streets were filled with the soldiers marching to and fro, and the usual quiet of the sacred day was entirely destroyed. It happened that one of the principal meeting-houses—as the churches were then called—was situated directly opposite to the town-house, and the devotions of the congregation during the hours of service were greatly interrupted by the martial sounds in the streets. The officers in command of the troops made no effort to mitigate the difficulty by avoiding unnecessary movements and noise, but seemed rather to take pleasure in aggravating the annoyance which their presence occasioned, as if they enjoyed the idea of parading their power, and domineering over a people who they knew hated them, but were utterly powerless to resist them.

THE EXCITEMENT CONTINUES

On Monday, the excitement of the people increased instead of diminishing. The merchants, when they came to the street, in business hours, found their exchange filled with soldiers—while guards stationed at the doors, with insolent looks and demeanor forbade their entrance. Troops were drawn up in different parts of the street, and the cannon were planted so as to command all the approaches. Sentinels were stationed, too, in different parts of the town, and the people were summoned by them as they went peaceably to and fro, engaged in their ordinary pursuits. All these things greatly incensed the people, and fanned the increasing flame.

INTERPOSITION OF GENERAL GAGE

The contest between the governor and the military authorities on one side, and the people of Boston on the other, in respect to quarters for the troops, was continued for some days. General Gage himself came on from New York to see what he could do toward arranging the difficulty. But he was no more successful than Governor Bernard had been, and at length, finding that the selectmen and the people of the town were resolute, and determined not to yield, he yielded himself, and hired a number of buildings sufficient for the purpose required, paying for them from his own military fund.

After this the excitement in some degree subsided. Still, as the Common—which was a general playground and place of recreation for the town—was covered with tents and guarded by sentinels, and as companies of soldiers were continually to be seen marching to and fro about the streets, from one to another of the different buildings in which the troops had been quartered, the source of irritation was continually kept open, and little collisions were frequently taking place between individual soldiers and the rude boys and other reckless persons encountered by them in the streets. The evil was increased in some measure by the peculiarly conspicuous style of uniform which the British soldiers wore, the color being a scarlet of so bright a hue as to arrest the eye of the spectator as far off as it could be seen, and to make a body of men wearing it stand out to the view in as marked a contrast as possible with the quietly-dressed townspeople around them.

There was an eccentric minister living in Boston at this time, named Matthew Byles. He was quite celebrated for his jokes and comic sayings of all kinds. One of his jokes related to these red-coated soldiers. He was walking with some of his friends when a company of the soldiers were marching by. "There," said he, "you have been a long time complaining of your grievances, and now, at last, you have got them red-dressed."

THE OFFICERS ATTEMPT TO CONCILIATE THE LADIES

After the lapse of some weeks or months spent in this way, the military men began to feel somewhat uncomfortable in their position—being shunned and avoided by the whole community, and looked upon with aversion and dislike as unwelcome intruders, if not as enemies. The officers finally attempted to conciliate the upper classes at least of the society of Boston, by giving a series of balls, parties, concerts and other social entertainments. They tried this plan faithfully for some time, but it did not succeed. There was a small circle of polite society, consisting of the families of the governor, the commissioners of the customs, the judges and some other official personages, whose places depended upon the king or upon the ministry in England, and whose sympathies were, consequently, all on the side of the military; but beyond this circle, the officers could not induce any of the ladies of consideration and influence to accept their invitations.

BURNING OF THE JAIL

There was one occasion, however, in which the soldiers really rendered an important service to the community—which was the only benefit, as some of the writers of the day alleged, that resulted from the measure of sending them to Boston—and that was on the occurrence of the accidental burning of the jail in the night, by which multitudes of the prisoners would have been burnt to death, had it not been for the very efficient aid which some of the soldiers rendered in rescuing them.

It was on the thirtieth of January—mid-winter—that the fire took place. The first alarm in the town arose from the people in the houses next to the jail being awakened by a great noise and commotion within the walls, accompanied by cries of fire. The external walls of the jail were of stone, but the inner partitions were of wood, strengthened and bound with iron bars and bolts. Before the people could collect, the inside of the building was all on fire. The outer door was soon opened, but, in the confusion, the keys of the rooms and passageways could not be found. The people tried to cut through the doors and partitions with axes, or to pry them open with crowbars, but everything had been so reinforced with iron that it was almost impossible to get the prisoners out. Still the people persevered, some toiling incessantly at the work of battering down and breaking through the interior petitions to rescue the prisoners, while the rest were fighting the fire.

Many of the soldiers assisted very effectively at the fire, though at first the people declined their aid, thinking, perhaps, that they could subdue the fire themselves. When, however, they found it growing very serious, they were glad to receive assistance. Some of the military men evinced a great deal of daring in the contest with the fire, and rendered great service both in rescuing the prisoners and in preventing the fire from extending. One of the captains—Captain Wilson—particularly distinguished himself. The commodore who commanded the fleet was present, and many of the other officers from the ships came. The sailors, too, brought an engine on shore from the *Romney* to play upon the fire.

As soon as the prisoners were rescued, the authorities of the town applied to the commander of the troops to send a small body of soldiers to guard them, until some other suitable arrangements could be made for them, and he did so. This was almost the only instance in which any friendly intercourse or cooperation took place between the authorities of the town and the English soldiers during all the time that they remained quartered in Boston.

THE COMMISSIONERS OF CUSTOMS

The five commissioners of customs, who, as has already been stated, were sent out some time previous to this, to superintend the collection of the revenue in Boston, and who had fled from the town to seek refuge on board the *Romney*, and afterward in the castle, at the time of the difficulty in respect to John Hancock's sloop, returned to town when the soldiers came, and assumed there a more lofty and imperious tone than ever. They lived in a very aristocratic and lordly style, made themselves quite inaccessible to those who desired from time to time to communicate with them—and seemed to entertain a feeling of contempt and hostility to the people of the province. They attempted, by their haughty and overbearing demeanor, to put down all who were suspected of being opposed to the measures of the government. At one time they dismissed a man from his office in the customs on account of a vote which he gave in the assembly. They wrote home to the ministry denouncing many of the most prominent men in Boston as rebels and traitors. Among others whom they thus denounced was James Otis, one of the most prominent and influential men in Boston at that day.

JAMES OTIS

James Otis was an eminent lawyer, and a man of great personal and political influence in the town. He was, however, a man of very ardent temperament, and he had assumed quite a prominent part on the side of the province, in the discussions which had taken place in respect to the right of Parliament to tax the colonies, and to that of the king to quarter troops upon them. In their letters home, the commissioners had denounced Otis, among others, as a rebel and traitor, who was aiming at producing a revolt of the colonies, and the dismemberment of the empire. These letters were afterward published, and in due time they came to Otis's knowledge. They filled his soul with indignation and rage.

OTIS'S IDEA OF HIS POSITION IN A LEGAL POINT OF VIEW

Otis considered it gross and malicious slander to accuse him of treason and rebellion. Neither he nor any of his compatriots, so far as we can judge from any evidence now attainable, had at this time any intention or even any wish to separate the colonies from the mother country. In their opposition to the measures of the government they considered themselves as acting entirely within the limits of their rights as British subjects, and as occupying precisely the same position as other British subjects in England had often done in their resistance to the encroachments of the crown on the liberties of the people. The simple question at issue between the government and the colonies—and this was strictly and purely a question of constitutional law—was whether the colonial legislatures were to be regarded as standing in the same relation to the people of the colonies, as the English Parliament did to the people at home. At home, the people had a body of representatives chosen by themselves, who were the constitutional guardians and defenders of their rights and liberties, against the encroachments of power. The colonists claimed that *their* representatives should exercise the same functions for them, and this the ministers of the king refused—they claiming that the home legislature was intrusted with this duty for the whole empire—for those who were not, as well as for those who were, directly represented in it.

This was the whole question in dispute. This being once settled, everything was settled; for it was an established principle of the British constitution, that the people of England could not be taxed, nor could any troops be organized and quartered in the kingdom, except by the consent of Parliament previously obtained; and if the colonial legislatures sustained the same relation to the people of the colonies that Parliament did to the people of England, then the taxing of the colonies and quartering troops upon them was illegal, for the consent of the legislatures had not been given. If, on the other hand, the colonial legislature did not sustain this relation, but if Parliament was to be considered as the guardian of the rights and liberties of the whole empire—then the taxing of the colonies, and the sending of troops among them was legal, for the English Parliament had given its consent to these measures.

Thus the question at issue was truly a legal one, and one on which loyal men might honestly differ, and lawfully discuss in any peaceable way; and the fact that any man took the opposite ground upon it from that occupied by his majesty's ministers for the time being, by no means made him a rebel and a traitor, however strenuously he might urge his opinion. It is not surprising, therefore, that Otis and the others thus accused felt extremely indignant at having such charges made against them.

Otis Advertises the Commissioners

One morning—it was on the Fourth of July, 1769—about a year after the arrival of the troops in Boston, the following advertisement appeared in the *Boston Gazette,* signed by Otis's name in full.

Advertisement

"Whereas, I have full evidence that Henry Hutton, Charles Paxton, William Burch and John Robinson, Esquires"—these were the names of the four commissioners of customs—"have frequently and lately treated the characters of all true Americans in a manner that is not to be endured, by privately and publicly representing them as traitors and rebels, and in a general combination to revolt against Great Britain, and whereas the said Henry, Charles, William and John, without the least provocation or color, have represented me by name as inimical to the rights of the crown, and disaffected to his majesty, to whom I annually swear, and am determined at all events to bear true and faithful allegiance; for all which general as well as personal abuse and insult satisfaction has been personally demanded and due warning given, but no sufficient answer obtained, these are humbly to desire the lords commissioners of his majesty's treasury, his principal secretaries of state, particularly my Lord Hillsboro"— these were the principal ministers of the crown in England that were connected with the management of colonial affairs—"and all others whom it may concern, or who may condescend to read this, to pay no kind of regard to any of the abusive representations of me or of my country, that may be transmitted by the said Henry, Charles, William and John or their confederates; for they are no more worthy of credit than those of Sir Francis Bernard, of Nettleham, Bart., or any of his cabal; which cabal may be well known from the papers in the House of Commons, and at every great office in England.

JAMES OTIS."

SIR FRANCIS BERNARD, OF NETTLEHAM, BART.

This Sir Francis Bernard, of Nettleham, Bart., of whom Otis speaks thus contemptuously as a man so notoriously unworthy of confidence or credit, was the governor of the province, of whom mention has been frequently made in the preceding pages. He was, however, not now any longer in office. He had become an object of such universal dislike and hostility in Massachusetts by his resolute persistence in his efforts to bring the province to submission, and by his haughty and overbearing demeanor, that he had been recalled, and Hutchinson, who had hitherto been lieutenant-governor, had been appointed to his place. Before recalling him, however, the ministry, in order to reward him for his zeal, and enable him to leave Boston in a species of triumph, had made him a baronet, and Otis, in his advertisement, gives him his title in full, and in a contemptuous and sarcastic manner.

ANGER OF THE COMMISSIONERS

The commissioners, on finding themselves thus insultingly posted in the public papers, considered it their turn to be filled with indignation and rage. The affair, of course, was the subject of a great deal of excitement during the day of the publication, and in the evening there resulted from it a personal collision between one of the commissioners and Mr. Otis. Mr. Otis went into a coffee-room in King Street, which stood where the Massachusetts Bank now stands, in the present State Street—and there, as it happened, he found Robinson, one of the commissioners, seated in company with a number of his friends. Robinson at once assailed Otis with opprobrious language, and undertook to pull his nose. On Otis's attempting to defend himself, Robinson began belaboring him with his cane, and a violent and protracted scuffle ensued. One of Otis's friends passing by at the time, rushed in and attempted to protect him, but he was but one among a large number, and could do nothing. After a while, however, the combatants were separated, and Otis was carried home, wounded, bleeding and very seriously injured.

Exactly what happened at this affray could never be precisely ascertained, as the persons present were all Robinson's friends, and they did all in their power to withhold evidence. Several stout sticks, really clubs, though in the form of canes, were found upon the floor after Otis was carried away, and also a scabbard of a sword. Otis had a deep wound in his head, too, which the surgeons said must have been made by some sharp instrument.

RESULTS OF THE ASSAULT UPON OTIS

This affair, of course, produced an intense excitement throughout the whole town. People naturally took sides according to their political predilections, the British party all justifying Robinson, and declaring that Otis had received only what he deserved, while the people of the province universally took part with Otis, and were aroused to a greater pitch of anger and resentment against the commissioners, and against the whole array of British influence in the colony than ever.

It was charged, and generally believed, that Robinson and his friends intended to assassinate Mr. Otis, and that they waylaid him in the coffeehouse for this end. He was, indeed, very seriously wounded. The gash in his head was very long in being healed, and when it was healed, it left a depression in which it was said a person might lay his finger. His mind, too, became afterward very seriously affected, and this was attributed by many persons, in a great measure, to the injuries which he had received.

THE ACTION FOR DAMAGES

Otis brought an action against Robinson in the courts, for assault and battery. The cause was protracted for some time, but it was finally decided in 1770. Robinson was found guilty, and sentenced to pay a sum equal to ten thousand dollars, in atonement for the injury which he had done. Otis, however, declined receiving this money, on the ground that his only motive for bringing the case before the courts was to establish legally, and to the satisfaction of the whole country, that Robinson was the aggressor. He offered, therefore, if Robinson, by his counsel—for he himself had left the country and returned to

England before the case was decided—would acknowledge his fault, and make proper apologies, to release him from all obligation to pay this money—which for those days was quite a large sum.

To this the counsel agreed, and he signed an acknowledgment in Robinson's name, fully admitting that he was the aggressor in the assault committed—that it was commenced "by his presumptuously attempting to take the said James Otis by the nose, and that this was the first assault which occasioned and brought on all the consequent insults, wounds and other injuries whereof the said James Otis complains. He, the said John Robinson, Esquire, was greatly in fault, is very sorry for his conduct and behavior that night toward the said James Otis, and asks the pardon of the said James Otis."

Thus the affair, so far as it was a personal matter between Otis and the commissioner, was at length amicably settled, but in respect to its influence upon public sentiment in widening the breach between the people of the colony and the government of the mother country, it was never settled. For the breach which it helped so effectually to widen was never closed.

CHAPTER VI
THE MIDDLE AND SOUTHERN
COLONIES

Opposition to the Measures of the Government
General throughout All the Colonies

In tracing the history of the separation of the American colonies from the mother country, our attention has been mainly occupied thus far by what took place in Boston. This is owing to the fact that it was in the province of Massachusetts, and more particularly in the old town of Boston, that the opposition to the measures of the British government was first fully and distinctly organized. Thus this province for a time seemed to take the lead; and then, besides this, the occurrences which took place in Boston were many of them of so personal and dramatic a character, that they have invested the contest, as it was waged there, with a special interest for the readers of history, and this has, perhaps, had the effect to draw to the proceedings in Massachusetts a still greater proportion of attention than they actually deserve.

During all the period of which we have been writing in the preceding chapter, substantially the same contest had been going on between the government of the mother country and several of the other provinces, and the provincial assemblies of New York, of Pennsylvania, of Virginia, of Georgia, and of several other colonies, had evinced a strong disposition to join with Massachusetts in resisting what they called the encroachments of the English government upon the rights of the people of America, who, as British subjects, were entitled to the same immunities and privileges as were enjoyed by the English people at home.

Alleged Trivialness of the Causes of the Quarrel

Those who espoused the cause of the government in this their quarrel with the colonies, were very prone to reproach the people of America with the utter trivialness, as well as unreasonableness, of the complaints which they made.

It is only the question, said they, first of a few cents tax on a small number of commodities, the total amount of which, if allowed to be collected without unnecessary expense and trouble, would be too small to produce any appreciable effect upon the wealth of the colony—and secondly, of the presence of a few hundred troops in the capital, who, if they had been allowed to establish themselves peaceably there, would not have molested the inhabitants in any way, and would never be called upon for any services except to aid the magistrates in the execution of the laws.

The Two Great Foundations of English Liberty

All this seems sufficiently plausible, but in reality it keeps the real point at issue entirely out of view, which was, whether the two great safeguards for the people against the despotism of kings, which the English had struggled in former times so earnestly to obtain, and which they now held so tenaciously for themselves, were likewise to be enjoyed by their fellow-countrymen in America. These two safeguards, as has been intimated in a former chapter, were these, namely:

First, that the king could raise no money from his realm without the consent and approval of the representatives of the people, both for the amount to be raised and the manner of raising it. And,

Secondly, that he could maintain no troops among them without the same consent and approval.

General Effect of These Limitations

It is plain that these two restrictions on the power of the king had the effect of entirely disarming him in respect to any conflict that he might have with his subjects. By retaining in their hands these powers of furnishing the sovereign with money, and allowing him men, they made him completely dependent upon them, and rendered it utterly impossibly for him to tyrannize over them.

Indeed, it is by these provisions that the real difference is established between an absolute and a limited monarchy. In an absolute monarchy, the king's power is in a great measure uncontrolled. In a limited monarchy like that of England, the king holds his power under the restrictions above specified, namely, that he can raise no money from his subjects, nor hold in command any troops among them, except by their own formal and special consent, expressed by the voice of their representatives. Under this system, his majesty may indeed wield great power in administering the government according to the wishes of his subjects, for they may then furnish him with men and money in great abundance; but in any attempt to tyrannize over them, or to go counter to their wishes in any way, he becomes utterly powerless, for they can at once cut off his supplies, both of money and of men.

PRACTICAL RESULT IN ENGLAND

The people of England have struggled very perseveringly for many centuries, and waged many long and sometimes bloody contests with their sovereigns, to get this system into full and complete operation, and it is at length so firmly established, that now for a long period all contests between the crown and the people have entirely ceased. The moment that it appears that a majority of the House of Commons are opposed to any system of policy adopted by the government of the king, his majesty never waits to have his supplies actually cut off, but at once gives up the contest, and changes his policy by changing his ministers. No ministry can remain in office a week after their general policy is condemned by a representative body that has power at any moment to cut off the supplies of men and money by which alone the government can be carried on.

Intentions of the English Government in Respect to America

Now both the government and the people of England were agreed that this was the true and proper system to govern the relations between a king and his subjects, nor did anyone wish to exempt the colonies in America from the operation of it. No one desired to make the royal power absolute in America, any more than in England, but all agreed that the restrictions upon it above described should exist in one case as well as in the other. The only question was, in whose hands the power of exercising this control should be placed. The English maintained that their Parliament should hold it for the whole empire, since, though the members were elected only by English voters, the body might be considered as in some sense representing the whole population of the empire. The colonists maintained, on the other hand, that these restrictions on the power of the crown over *them,* should be held by their own direct representatives, that is, by the *colonial legislatures,* and refused to admit that the British Parliament was qualified to represent the interests, or to act in the name, of any portion of the empire except the people who had a voice in choosing them.

This was the real question at issue, and the colonists saw, in the attempt to tax them, first by the Stamp Act and afterward by the duties on the five articles of merchandise, and the quartering of troops among them, without first obtaining the sanction of their own representatives to those measures, only the first occasions on which these great questions came up practically for decision.

Action of Virginia

The various provinces in America which have since been so closely united as states of the Union, were at this time, it must be remembered, wholly distinct from each other, and the British government deemed it a matter of very great political importance to keep them thus distinct. They accordingly considered any attempt on the part of the different provinces to combine together, or to unite their action in any way, as a high misdemeanor. The colonists themselves were for a time very cautious in respect to any measures which might indicate an attempt to combine their strength. They were obliged to be satisfied with *concurrent,* instead of *combined,* action. The various legislatures, however, of the more southern colonies, each by its own independent measures, began soon to take a decided stand in sustaining Massachusetts in the position she had assumed, of resistance to the pretensions of the English ministers to govern the colonies through the action of Parliament, instead of through their own direct representatives. Among these southern colonies Virginia took the lead.

LORD BOTETOURT

The governor of Virginia at this time was Lord Botetourt. He was an upright, honorable and conscientious man, and seemed to be sincerely interested in promoting the welfare and prosperity of his colony—with the understanding, however, that the views and intentions of the home government, in respect to the subjection of the colony to the authority of Parliament, were sustained and carried into effect. He was, indeed, especially selected for the post of governor of Virginia on account of his possessing many excellent qualities which would be likely to give him great popularity and influence among the colonists, and so greatly increase his power to thwart the rising opposition to the policy of the government in America, and to carry the policy into effect.

ENGLISH IDEAS OF THE DISPLAY OF POMP AND PARADE AS AN AUXILIARY OF GOVERNMENT

The English are accustomed to attach much importance to the imposing effect of outward show in impressing upon the people a due sense of the majesty of law. In accordance with this idea, they invest the sovereign with all imaginable symbols of majesty and grandeur, and accompany the proceedings of government, where they come under the direct observation of the people, with ceremonies, and pageants, and displays innumerable. The same principle extends in a degree through all subordinate ranks and departments of government.

The magistrates are escorted to church sometimes by a guard of officials in antique and grotesque costumes. The dignity of the judges on the bench is sustained by black robes, and great gray wigs, which give to all men alike, the venerable aspect of wisdom, gravity and years. Even the lawyers at the bar wear a characteristic costume, to assist in impressing their clients with a sense of their dignity and importance.

All such things in this country would awaken only a feeling of ridicule. Besides, according to American ideas, it is not desirable to invest the agents of power with any factitious prestige. If a judge, for example, cannot inspire a sufficient respect for his decisions by the actual weight of his character—his justice, his learning, his intrinsic dignity and impartiality—we do not think it worthwhile to attempt to eke out the deficiency by means of silken robes and a gray wig.

POMP AND PARADE AFFECTED BY LORD BOTETOURT

Lord Botetourt, notwithstanding his good sense and his other excellent qualities, seems to have entertained the idea of strengthening the impression which he wished to make upon the natives of his province in respect to the majesty and grandeur of the power whose agent and instrument he was, by the pomp and parade which he could display. He provided himself with a splendid mansion which he called the palace. He affected great state when he appeared in public. He introduced all the forms and ceremonies, in opening the legislative assembly, that are practiced in the case of the Parliament in England, which, though somewhat tedious and inconvenient, are well enough retained there, since they have come down by regular transmission in that assembly from time immemorial—but which appear ridiculous when introduced anew among such a plain, practical and unpretending body of men as a provincial legislature in a new country. The governor, however, in pursuing this course, only carried out what he knew to be the wish and intention of the government at home. The king himself, when he was coming to America, made him a present of a splendid state coach, and on the opening of the legislature, Lord Botetourt caused himself to be taken to the hall in this coach, drawn by a team of eight milk-white horses, and attended by a gay cavalcade. The people in

The state carriage.

the street looked curiously upon this pageantry, as it passed, without, however, seeming to be specially overawed by it, while many of the more serious men in the province were much displeased with it.

Conciliatory Tone Adopted by the Governor in His Opening Message

The governor, in opening the session of the legislature, adopted a very conciliatory tone, and he evinced so cordial a feeling of goodwill toward the people of the province, and so earnest a desire to promote their prosperity and welfare, that he made an extremely favorable impression upon everyone. The assembly, when left to themselves, after receiving the governor's message voted a reply to it, which was of a very respectful and complimentary character. They warmly reciprocated the kind wishes of the governor, and expressed sentiments of firm and faithful loyalty to the king. These civilities having been interchanged, and the session being thus regularly opened, the members set themselves at work in earnest to consider and to act upon the great questions connected with the alarming state of public affairs. The result of their deliberations indicated that neither the imposing show, nor the flattering civilities of the governor, had had the effect of making them swerve from what they considered their duty.

The Virginia Resolutions

A series of resolutions were brought in, in which all the various points of dispute that had arisen between the home government and the province of Massachusetts were taken up in order, and a position of distinct and decided opposition to the course pursued by the government was assumed in respect to every one of them. These points were the following. The resolutions declared,

1. That the sole right of imposing taxes on the inhabitants of the colony of Virginia, was then, and ever had been, legally and constitutionally vested in the *provincial assembly*.

2. That it was lawful for the people of the colonies, at any and at all times, to petition his majesty for a redress of grievances.

3. That in case of any infraction of the rights of any of the colonies, it was the privilege and right of the people thereof to endeavor to procure the *concurrence of his majesty's other colonies* in dutiful addresses, praying the royal interposition in behalf of their violated rights.

4. That all trials for treason, or for any other crime, committed or alleged to have been committed in the colony, ought to be conducted before his majesty's *colonial courts.*

This was in allusion to the intention which had been declared by the British government to cause the chief leaders in the opposition to the government at Boston to be arrested and conveyed to England, to be tried on the charge of treason there, where they could be under the direct eye of the ministers themselves, and in the hands of courts and juries whose predilections and sympathies would be almost all against them.

The resolution on this fourth point went on to declare, "that the transportation of any person, suspected or accused of any crime whatsoever committed in the colony, for trial in another country, is derogatory to the rights of British subjects, inasmuch as the accused is thereby deprived of the inestimable privilege of being tried by a jury of his vicinity, as well as of the power of procuring witnesses at his trial."

These resolutions, after full discussion, were passed unanimously. The assembly also, at the same time, framed an address to the king, in which, while they gave to his majesty strong assurances of loyalty to his crown and attachment to his person, they expressed a deep and firm conviction that the complaints of *all his American subjects* were well founded.

This last expression was likely to be particularly obnoxious to the ministers, for by assuming thus to speak for and in the name of the people of all the colonies, the assembly seemed to take another step toward some general banding together of the people of America for common and united action in resistance to the government, which the ministers looked upon with abhorrence, as a treasonable conspiracy, and which they dreaded as the source of the greatest danger.

The Governor Dissolves the Assembly

As soon as the governor was informed of these proceedings, he was much displeased, and not a little alarmed. On the next day after the resolutions were passed, he suddenly presented himself in the hall, and addressed the assembly as follows:

"Mr. Speaker and Gentlemen:
"I have heard of your resolutions and augur ill of their effects. You have made it my duty to dissolve you. You are dissolved accordingly."

This act, of course, put a sudden stop to the proceedings of the body; for, by the fundamental law of the province, the legislature, though the members of it were elected by the people, was only to be convened at the summons of the governor, and the duration of its sessions, and even of its existence, depended wholly on his will.

The legislature obeyed at once the mandate of the governor. They at once closed the session and left the hall. They, however, proceeded immediately to a private house, and there reorganized, not as a legislative assembly, for they admitted that the governor's decree of dissolution had deprived them of all power to act in that capacity, but only as an association of private citizens. They, however, appointed their late speaker to be the presiding officer of the meeting, under the name of moderator.

This meeting, after some consultation and debate as to the course of proceeding which they should adopt, at length drew up a written agreement, which they all signed, pledging themselves thenceforth not to import, purchase or use any articles of British manufacture. They also caused copies of the agreement to be printed, and made arrangements for sending them to all the towns and villages of the province, in order that they might be signed as extensively as possible by the whole population, and the market for British goods in the province be entirely closed, until the government should abandon their attempts to deprive the people of the colonies of what they deemed to be their constitutional rights.

The governor, though he could by a word dissolve the provincial assembly, had no power in respect to a meeting of private gentlemen, and so he could not interfere with these proceedings at all—but he was made very indignant by them, and immediately reported the facts to the government at home.

THE EXAMPLE OF VIRGINIA IS FOLLOWED BY ALL THE SOUTHERN COLONIES

As fast as intelligence of the firm stand which Virginia had taken spread through the country, the excitement of the controversy was greatly increased, and the determination of the people of the different colonies to make common cause in their resistance to the claims of the ministry and of Parliament to govern and to tax them from London, was greatly strengthened. The legislatures of the different provinces immediately began to adopt the same measures that the Virginia assembly had initiated.

The assembly of South Carolina passed a vote refusing to provide accommodations for British troops, thus formally sustaining Massachusetts in the position which she had taken, and they also passed a series of resolutions, the same substantially as those of Virginia. The Virginia resolutions were also brought into the assemblies of New York, Delaware, Maryland, North Carolina and Georgia, and passed in them all with great unanimity. In North Carolina, the governor, on learning what the assembly had done, at once followed Governor Botetourt's example, and dissolved the body. The members then immediately did as those of the Virginia legislature had done. They reassembled at a private house, as a company of private persons, and passed resolutions binding themselves not to import, purchase or use any goods of British manufacture, and recommending to the people of the province universally to come to the same determination.

The great mass of the people in all the colonies responded very readily to the appeal, and they formed clubs and associations in a great many places, to prevent the use of articles of English manufacture of every kind, and to encourage the production of substitutes for them in America.

A MINORITY OPPOSED TO THESE PROCEEDINGS

Although the great mass of the people in all the colonies joined at once and very cordially in these measures, there was still quite a large minority, especially in all the great cities, that strongly opposed them. This minority consisted mainly of public officers who held their offices by appointment from the home government, and of wealthy men in the principal cities and towns, who belonged to the conservative class that are always interested in sustaining any existing power. These persons, of course, resisted the attempt to prevent the introduction of British goods, and declared that they would purchase and use such articles as they pleased, without any regard to the resolutions and edicts of meetings and clubs. So they attempted to go on importing and using the articles as before.

But this produced such a storm of indignation from the community around them, that they soon gave up importing the goods publicly, but attempted to do it by stealth. Then the clubs appointed committees to watch the arrival of every ship, and to ascertain what goods were on board, and to whom they were consigned; and when they ascertained that any persons were importing any of the prohibited articles, they published their names, and thus brought the secret to light.

These proceedings, of course, led to a great deal of difficulty and ill-will. The government officials did all in their power to protect those who wished to continue the importations of British goods, but the community was so nearly unanimous against them, and found so many means of persecuting and annoying them, which it was beyond the reach of the government to arrest, that the dissentients were at length compelled to give up the contest, and in the end the commerce with England was so nearly cut off that the British merchants and manufacturers began to suffer very severely, and to call upon the government at home not to persist in a policy which was thus depriving them of so many of their best customers. This was precisely the result that the colonists hoped and expected that their action would produce.

THE LOTTERY TICKETS

Among the other restrictions upon the trade with England which agreements made by the colonists among themselves included, there was one that was quite curious and somewhat characteristic of the times, and that was the trade in lottery tickets. Almost all governments in those days authorized lotteries, and many employed the system directly as a governmental measure, considering it a legitimate mode of raising money for any useful public purpose. The English had drawn a great deal of money from America in this way for tickets sold here—a very considerable portion of the whole number of tickets in the British lotteries having been taken by the people of the provinces. The sale of these tickets was now included in the prohibition to deal in British commodities, and the cutting off of the American market interfered seriously with the plans and calculations of the managers of the lotteries, and thus added them also to the number of the dissatisfied and complaining at home.

THE PRIDE OF THE GOVERNMENT FORBIDS CONCESSION

The proceedings of the legislature of Virginia and of the other southern colonies which have been described in this chapter, were taking place during the same period that the difficulties occurred in Massachusetts, as related in the last; and the combined effect of the restrictions on the trade in producing discontent and dissatisfaction among the merchants and manufacturers in England, and in increasing the embarrassment which the government found in dealing with the formidable spirit of resistance which was manifesting itself through all the colonies, finally convinced the government that they would be compelled to yield. They, however, persisted so long, and yielded at last so partially, that they failed to conciliate the colonies, or to do anything effectual toward healing the breach.

It is not surprising that the pride of a government controlled by a haughty aristocracy like that of England, should revolt strongly against being driven to concession by communities of plebeian settlers in the American woods; and if personal as well as national pride had been involved in the question, that is, if the same men were required to consent to a repeal of the measures, that had been the original enactors of them, it is probable they would never have been repealed. But during all this period, continual changes were taking place in Parliament and especially in the ministry—so that new men were called upon to act from time to time, who were not personally responsible for the measures which had produced the difficulty. Still, their national, or as perhaps it should be called, their *governmental* pride, was involved, and they evinced a great unwillingness to yield to the pressure. Even when a ministry at last came in that admitted that the policy which had been pursued was wrong, and ought not to have been instituted, yet still, as they maintained, since it had been instituted, and had met with such factious, if not absolutely treasonable, resistance, the government could not without disgrace recede from its ground until all such resistance had ceased.

The colonies, however, on their part, declared that they would not withdraw their measures of resistance until the grievances were actually redressed; and thus for many months the difficulty seemed to be hopelessly locked.

THE GOVERNMENT FINALLY YIELDS

At length, however, the government, finding that the people of the colonies were growing every month more and more resolute and determined in their resistance, and that the difficulties and embarrassments of their position were continually increasing, concluded to yield, or at least to pretend to yield. They gave notice to the various agents of the colonies that were residing in London, that they had determined on complying with the wishes of the colonies, and soon afterward, they sent a circular letter to all the provinces, saying that the ministers had resolved on recommending to Parliament at its next session, to repeal the taxes on glass, lead, paper and colors, on the ground of "said duties being laid contrary to the true principles of commerce, and that they entertained no design to propose to Parliament to lay any further taxes upon America for the purpose of raising a revenue."

THE COLONISTS FAR FROM BEING SATISFIED WITH THIS DECLARATION

The news of this circular was at first received in the colonies with much joy, but the more prudent and cautious men soon observed that the article of *tea* was not included in the list of those from which the duty was to be withdrawn, and that the ministry, by the very terms in which they announced their intention to repeal the other taxes, did not at all relinquish their pretended right to tax the colonies, but only proposed for the time being to waive the exercise of the right. Thus, in respect to the real question at issue, no concession was made, and it became the prevalent opinion in America that the government did not intend at all to abandon the ground which they had taken, but only to temporize with the question in order to escape from the present embarrassment, with a view of reasserting their power on some more convenient occasion, when circumstances should perhaps render it more difficult for the colonists to resist. They determined, therefore, not to relax their efforts, and declared, through their legislatures, that they would not return to the purchase and use of British manufactures until the government had repealed all the taxes which had been laid by authority of Parliament on the people of the colonies.

Things were in this state when an incident occurred in Boston which aroused anew the excitement of all the people of the country, and made it greatly more intense than it had ever been before. This incident was a collision between the military in Boston and some of the people in the town, in which several persons lost their lives. The affair received by the colonists the name of the Boston Massacre, and the circumstances connected with it will be related in full in the next chapter.

CHAPTER VII
THE BOSTON MASSACRE

A MISNOMER

The occurrence which forms the subject of this chapter is called here the Boston Massacre, as it is by that name that it is known in history. The affair was, in itself perhaps, of no very great importance, as it was simply a collision between the soldiery and the populace, in the streets of Boston, by which a few not especially valuable lives were lost. And as to the criminality of the deed, the authors of it were afterward nearly all of them acquitted by the colonial courts and juries themselves.

The occurrence, however, produced so great and widespread an excitement at the time, and contributed so much to arouse the resentment and increase the hostility of the colonies against the mother country, and to hasten the final outbreak, that it has always occupied a very conspicuous place among the events which marked the history of the times.

SCENE OF THE MASSACRE

The scene of the massacre was what was then King Street, but is now State Street, in Boston. It took place at a short distance below the building which now stands in the middle of the street at the junction of State and Washington streets. This building, which subsequently became the City Hall, and is now devoted to private uses, was then the State House; and the vicinity of it was the scene of many very interesting events and occurrences in those days. The time of the massacre, so-called, was the 5th of March, 1770.

GREAT INCREASE OF HOSTILE FEELING BETWEEN THE CITIZENS AND THE SOLDIERS

From the time when the British troops had first been quartered in Boston, the ill-will which existed between the citizens and the soldiers had been gradually increasing until it had at length reached a degree of exasperation which was of a very threatening character. Perhaps there were never a set of men on earth worse than the enlisted soldiers of the British army of those days, and in choosing the regiments to send to Boston, the government does not at any rate seem to have looked for men less violent and depraved than the average of their class. There were two regiments—the Fourteenth and the Twenty-ninth. The men of the Twenty-ninth made themselves particularly obnoxious to the people of Boston, by their overbearing, violent and reckless behavior in the streets and in their casual intercourse with the people of the town. The people themselves, doubtless, especially those of the lower classes, returned insult for insult and injury for injury; and thus quarrels and collisions were continually occurring, each of which increased the general excitement, until it was no longer safe to walk the streets, and a general outbreak and conflict seemed imminent every day.

COLLISIONS BETWEEN THE SOLDIERS AND CITIZENS IN NEW YORK

While these things were occurring in Boston, similar scenes were witnessed in New York. There the soldiers attempted to cut down a liberty pole in the park. The men and boys assembled in haste to defend the pole, and three times the soldiers were repulsed. The fourth time the soldiers succeeded, and cut down the pole. For two days after this the streets of New York were filled with parties of citizens and soldiers fighting each other. Of course, the military authorities on the one side, and the civil on the other, made a certain degree of effort to restrain these riots, but for some time without success. The soldiers, of course, were not armed, but fought like the others, with clubs and stones. In the end, it seems they were beaten, being of course greatly outnumbered, and then the town boys bought a piece of ground near the junction of Broadway and the Bowery, where they put up another liberty pole, taller than the one that had been cut down—setting it very deep in the earth, and strengthening it at the foot with bars and bands of iron to such a degree as to make the work of cutting through it so difficult and tedious, that the soldiers could not possibly hope to accomplish it before a force could be assembled to drive them away.

Tidings of These Occurrences in Boston

Of course, the tidings of these occurrences soon reached Boston, and the effect was, as may easily be imagined, greatly to increase the excitement, and to make both the soldiers and the people of the town more eager than ever for a combat there. The townspeople were enthusiastic in their eagerness to emulate the prowess of their New York fellow combatants in giving the soldiers a beating—while the soldiers were exasperated at the defeat of their comrades in New York, and were burning with a vehement desire to avenge it.

Hostile Feelings toward the Friends and Partisans of the Government

The hostile feeling which the people manifested toward the soldiers extended to all those who were supposed to sympathize with the government in their attempts to tax the colonies, and to force them to submission by the presence of an armed force. In this way a number of quarrels and collisions occurred which sometimes led to serious consequences.

In one case, there was a certain merchant who insisted on selling tea secretly, contrary to an alleged agreement that he had made not to sell any. One morning, the people, in passing by his house, saw a strong stake set up before his door with various significant symbols and inscriptions upon it, among the rest the figure of a hand pointing to the house as in derision. The people gathered around. Among them was one of the neighbors, a man named Richardson, who was a friend of the merchant and of the government, and he, seeing a countryman coming along with a cart, asked him to drive his cart against the stake and break it down.

The bystanders interposed and would not allow him to do it. Richardson remonstrated and attempted to lead the horse against the stake himself. A quarrel ensued, the end of which was that a number of boys chased Richardson home, by throwing stones at him; and when they reached his house, they continued to throw stones at the house. Richardson then came out with a gun and fired into the crowd. One of the boys was killed. He was the son of a poor German, and about eleven years old.

Of course, this affair produced an intense and universal excitement. The people gave the boy a public burial, and the funeral was conducted with great ceremony. Six of the school-fellows of the deceased bore the pall, and a company of five hundred children walked in procession before the bier. The name of the boy was Christopher Snider, and he was afterward sometimes called the first martyr in the cause of American independence, as his life was the first one that was lost in these preliminary struggles.

There was one circumstance which contributed a great deal to make the townspeople more bold and reckless in their street quarrels with the soldiers, and this was that martial law had not been proclaimed in Boston, so that the town was still under the control of the regular civil government; and according to the principles of public law, no military officer could, under any circumstances, order the men to fire upon the citizens, except when called upon to do so by a properly authorized civil officer.

Thus, when the soldiers were off duty, they went about the streets unarmed; and when they were on duty, as for instance when they were on guard, or were marching in squads or companies through the streets, the people knew, or rather supposed, that however much they taunted or insulted them, the officer in command would not dare to order his men to fire upon them.

COMMENCEMENT OF THE DIFFICULTY WHICH LED TO THE MASSACRE

The desire of the soldiers and the citizens to find an occasion for a fight was pretty soon gratified in consequence of an occurrence which took place at a ropewalk in the town—the blame of which, in the first instance, rests wholly, as it would seem, upon a townsman. A soldier of the Twenty-ninth regiment—the one which was the most obnoxious to the people—was passing peaceably by the ropewalk, when one of the workmen, looking out at a window, accosted him, and asked him if he did not want a job—the soldiers being not unwilling, it seems, to earn a little money now and then by working for the townspeople when off duty.

The soldier answered yes, whereupon the man gave him an indecent and outrageously insulting rejoinder, and broke into a fit of coarse and derisive laughter.

It was a wanton and wholly gratuitous insult on the part of the ropewalk man.

The soldier was, of course, exceedingly angry. He challenged the workman to come out and fight him. The workman came out, and he and the soldier had a fight with their fists in the street. The soldier was beaten, and the workman went back among his comrades, who had assembled at the door to witness the affair, exulting in his victory.

The soldier then went off to the barracks, but soon returned, bringing with him a party of his comrades, all full of excitement and burning with revenge. The rope-makers came out to meet them, at the same time sending messengers to other ropewalks calling upon the men there to come to their aid.

The soldiers were beaten in this second rencontre, being probably outnumbered, and retreated. But they only retreated to obtain reinforcements, and they afterward came back to the ropewalk again and again, each time in greater numbers—but finding at each attack that the rope-makers had been more and more fully reinforced. The affair was now becoming serious, but by this time Mr. Gray, the owner of the ropewalk, having heard what was going on, came with a number of friends to the spot, and after a great deal of trouble and difficulty, succeeded in drawing off his men and putting an end to the quarrel for that day.

This affair took place on Friday, the 2d of March; three days before the massacre, which occurred on Monday, the 5th.

EXCITEMENT ON SATURDAY

The excitement which spread through the town in consequence of this affair became very great on the following day. The soldiers, who had been so repeatedly beaten, declared that the matter should not end there.

They resolved that the honor of the regiment required that the townsmen should be yet conquered and humbled. The commander of the regiment, in some sense, took their part, as it was very natural that he should do. He appealed to Governor Hutchinson—then the acting governor of the colony—and maintained that the responsibility of commencing the disturbance rested with the ropewalk man who had so insultingly repelled the soldier, civilly applying to be employed. Mr. Gray, on being applied to, acknowledged the justice of this, and dismissed the man from his employment. This, however, did not satisfy the soldiers. They had been beaten by the town-boys, and nothing could restore the tarnished honor of the regiment but to give them a good beating in return.

They determined to do this on Monday, and they spent Saturday in laying their plans, and preparing clubs and other such weapons as they could procure. For of course when off duty they were not allowed to bear their regimental arms.

ATTITUDE OF THE COLONIAL AND MILITARY AUTHORITIES

While the excitement was thus rapidly extending, and both the townsmen and the soldiers were eager for another fight, it would seem that neither the officers in command of the troops on the one side, nor the civil authorities of the town or of the colony on the other, were as sincere and earnest in their efforts to prevent any farther disturbance as they might have been. The officers, although they would do nothing to encourage the men, were still probably not unwilling that they should have an opportunity to retrieve their credit, and teach the insolent townsmen, whom they themselves hated and despised as much as the soldiers did, a useful lesson. Accordingly, while they did not allow the men to go armed with deadly weapons, they left them at liberty all day on Saturday and Sunday, and late into the night, to go and come as they pleased through the streets, and form their plans and make their preparations for renewing the conflict without any molestation.

The authorities of the town, too, while of course they did not wish to have the hostility between the troops and the people proceed to too great an extremity, seem not to have desired that it should be too suddenly or too entirely allayed. They wished to have the soldiers removed to the castle, and to this end they were willing to have it fully appear that their presence in the town was entirely inconsistent with the peace and good order of the community. Of course, the continuance of these riots and disturbances tended to show that they were right, and while they would do nothing to encourage them, it was not to be expected that they would make any special or extraordinary efforts to suppress them, since by so doing they would show that the evils connected with the presence of the soldiers could be controlled, and of course that there was no serious objection to their remaining where they were.

Accordingly, after some ordinary precautions had been taken, the council met on Monday and passed a resolve that the town would never be safe from quarrels between the soldiers and the inhabitants, so long as the soldiers should be quartered among them. They immediately communicated these resolutions to the military authorities.

DELIBERATE ARRANGEMENTS MADE BY THE SOLDIERS

It would seem that some of the soldiers had formed the plan for a great combat between them and the people of the town on Monday evening, and fully expected that great numbers would be killed; for they not only, in many instances, uttered this determination, with suppressed but angry threats and imprecations, but they took pains especially to send word to many persons, who were supposed to be in sympathy with the British government, and whom they accordingly considered their friends, and notify them of the impending danger, and warn them to be on their guard. These warnings were given on Saturday and Sunday. It was not generally known at the time, that such warnings were given, but afterward, when testimony was regularly taken in respect to the affair, these facts with others came to light.

Examples of the Warnings Given

One of the witnesses, for example, who were afterward brought forward when the affair came to be legally investigated, testified that she was residing in the family of a certain Amos Thayer, and that a soldier came to the house on Saturday evening. "The soldier," as the witness went on to state, "desiring to speak with Mr. Thayer, was told by his sister, Mrs. Mary Thayer, that her brother was engaged and could not be spoken with. The soldier then said, 'Your brother, as you call him, is a man I have a great regard for, and I came on purpose to tell him to keep in his house; for before Tuesday night at twelve o'clock there will be a great deal of bloodshed and a great many lives lost.'

"He said, moreover, to Mrs. Thayer, that he came with this warning out of particular regard to her brother, to advise him to keep in his house, for then he would be out of harm's way. He added, 'Your brother knows me very well. My name is Charles Malone.' He then went away."

Another witness named Matthew Adams testified that he was sent early on Monday evening to a house where a certain corporal of the Twenty-ninth regiment had his quarters, and there saw the corporal and his wife, and also a young fifer, of the same regiment. After he had delivered his errand and was coming away, "The corporal," he says, "called him back, and desired him with great earnestness to go home to his master's house as soon as his business was over, and not to be abroad on any account, especially on that night, for the soldiers were determined to be revenged on the ropewalk people, and that much mischief would be done. Upon which, the fifer added that he hoped to God they would burn the town down. On this, he left the house, but the corporal called after him again, and begged he would mind what he said to him."

These and other similar testimonies, which were taken subsequently, were held to prove that there was a preconcerted plan formed among the soldiers, particularly of the Twenty-ninth regiment, to make a general attack upon the townspeople on Monday night, with a deliberate intention to kill as many as possible of them and to burn the town. It is evident that they do not really prove this, as the preliminary threats and denunciations of angry men in such cases as these, always go far in advance of their real designs; and then, moreover, the warnings given by the persons referred to in the depositions may have been prompted by the surmises and fears of timid or excited individuals, rather than by their knowledge of what was actually resolved upon.

GREAT EXCITEMENT ON MONDAY EVENING

However this may be, the whole town was in a state of great and intense excitement on Monday evening. It was a bright moonlight night, but there had been a fall of snow during the day, and the streets were covered to the depth of nearly a foot. Through this snow groups of men and boys were parading the streets, talking defiantly about the soldiers, and insulting those they met, calling them lobsters, and bloody backs, in allusion to the red coats which form so conspicuous a feature of the British uniform. The soldiers, too, who were allowed their usual liberty by the officers on that night, were out in small parties, and various petty collisions occurred, which, though attended by no immediately serious consequences, added to the prevailing excitement.

Many of the petty officers who were thus sauntering about with the soldiers wore their side arms, which consisted of bayonets, cutlasses and similar arms; and with these, in many instances, they made threatening thrusts at persons whom they met, and even struck blows with the flat of the weapon, but without doing any serious harm. In many cases they had some excuse for these outrages in the opprobrious or insulting words that the town-boys addressed to them as they passed; but at other times they were mere wanton expressions of their defiance and hate, and of their desire to bring on a conflict.

THE SENTINELS

Here and there at different posts sentinels were stationed as usual, and these were armed. These men, however, could not fire upon the people, however great the provocation, without an order from a superior officer, and, as has already been stated, no officer could order any soldier to fire, unless authorized to do so by the civil magistracy—except, indeed, in cases of immediate and urgent personal danger—as for example, if the townspeople were to come suddenly upon them and attack them with firearms, or with other deadly weapons, so as to put them in immediate danger of their lives. The people of the town knew this very well, and they felt sure that they might taunt and insult even an armed sentinel on his post as much as they pleased, and yet he would not dare to fire upon them unless they actually attempted to lay hands upon him. So they became, in many instances, very insolent and abusive.

One of these sentinels was stationed opposite the front of the custom-house, which stood near what is now the corner of State and Exchange streets; and while he was at his post, observing the various groups of men and boys in the street before him, he saw an officer passing, and a boy—it was a certain barber's boy named Edward Garrick—following him and calling out to him to pay for having his hair dressed at his master's shop, and telling the bystanders that there was a man so mean that he would not pay his barber.

The sentinel immediately stepped forward to the boy, and calling to him, said:

"Turn round here and let me see your face."

The boy turned round, saying that he was not ashamed to show his face to anybody in the world.

Upon this, the sentinel gave him a blow on the head with the butt of his musket, which sent him reeling and staggering into the street, and almost stunned him.

MURRAY'S BARRACKS

A large body of soldiers were quartered in barracks called Murray's barracks, which were situated near the end of Washington

Street—at that part of the street which was then called Cornhill—near its junction with Dock Square. These barracks were full of soldiers, and in the streets and lanes in the vicinity of them there began to congregate excited groups of people, who, as they passed to and fro, mingled more or less with the soldiers, the various parties, as they encountered each other, exchanging insults, imprecations and threats, and sometimes even blows. In the immediate vicinity of the barracks, and around the doors, were a great number of excited soldiers, making preparations apparently for a fight. A few were armed with bayonets and cutlasses, but most of them were only provided with the weapons of a mob—clubs and bludgeons, though some it seems for weapons had taken shovels and tongs. There were several subaltern officers that appeared among these men from time to time, some of whom, according to the testimony afterward given, were endeavoring to quiet the men, and induce them to go inside the barracks—though there was one who eagerly encouraged them, and urged them on. His voice could be heard in the midst of all the uproar and confusion calling out, "Turn out, boys! I'll stand by you! Go at 'm! Stick 'm! Knock 'm down. Run your bayonets through 'm! I'll stand by you!"

There were some persons of respectability and influence in the town who came at this time to the barracks, and urged the officer in command to call the men in. But the officer replied that the soldiers had been insulted by the people of the town, and it was the duty of the people first to retire. If they would disperse, then he would call in the soldiers.

MESSAGE FROM KING STREET

While things were in this state at the barracks a boy came running from King Street with news of the sentinel's having knocked a boy down with his musket, and calling upon the crowd to go to the rescue of him. Hereupon there was a great rush from the neighborhood of the barracks into King Street, and very soon the sentinel there was confronted by a crowd of some hundred wild and angry men and boys, who derided him, hooted him, threw snowballs at him, and did everything they possibly could to exasperate him and drive him to frenzy. He flourished his gun and made thrusts at them with his bayonet to keep them off, and pretended to make ready to fire. This only caused the mob to redouble their outcries and shouts of defiance and derision. They dared the old bloody back to fire, and pressed closer and closer upon him.

THE SENTINEL SENDS FOR HELP

The sentinel's post was in front of the building which was used as a custom-house, but which was also the residence of a family that had charge of the premises, and contained, moreover, the rooms occupied by the commissioners of customs, spoken of in a former chapter. The sentinel, finding himself so hardly pressed, turned and went quickly to the door of the custom-house and gave a thundering rap with the knocker. A person came to the door and opened it a little way. The sentinel said a word to him, and then the door was shut suddenly and the sentinel came back to his post.

A CORPORAL AND A FILE OF MEN

There was a guardhouse not far distant, where a small number of men were stationed, as usual in a town occupied by troops, consisting of the men necessary to relieve the sentinels on duty, from time to time, and to act as occasion might require in any sudden emergency. In a few minutes after the application of the sentinel to the door of the custom-house, a corporal and a file of men, with a captain of the regiment following them—Captain Preston by name—were seen marching rapidly down the street, the soldiers with bayonets fixed and presented, and the officers flourishing their cutlasses to drive the people out of their way. In one or two instances they had rude encounters with persons whom they met, though no one was seriously hurt by them. In this manner they marched rapidly on until they reached the post of the sentinel, and here they were at once drawn up, in a sort of semicircle, and presenting their bayonets toward the crowd of the people in the street, they assumed an attitude of resolute defiance. They were but half a dozen men against a hundred, but they were armed with gunpowder, lead and steel, while the mob of yelling men and boys before them had nothing to oppose to these deadly weapons but sticks and snowballs.

THE CRY OF FIRE

As soon as this maneuver had been executed, and the file of men had taken their position, the men and boys gathered around them, coming up as near as they dared to the points of the bayonets, and there filled the air with their taunting cries and fierce invectives, calling the soldiers all sorts of opprobrious names and daring them to fire. "Fire! Fire!" they cried. "Fire if you dare!"

A cry of fire soon began to be raised in the adjoining streets, and very soon the bells began to ring an alarm. Whether this alarm arose accidentally from the calls of the men and boys addressed to the soldiers, or whether some persons in the interest of the rioters raised the cry for the purpose of calling a greater number of the townspeople to the spot, does not certainly appear. At any rate, the alarm became general throughout the town, and multitudes of people came out from their houses, and ran along the streets asking where was the fire. Some of them were soon informed that there was no fire, but that a fight was going on between the military and the townspeople in King Street, and all, whether so informed or not, following the current which was everywhere setting in that direction, soon found their way to the scene of the difficulty. As they drew near to the spot, they heard the reports of musketry, and on turning into the street, they found the men and boys retreating in all directions, a portion of them bringing with them the bodies of their companions, some dead and some mortally wounded.

THE FIRING OF THE MILITARY ON THE CROWD

The soldiers had fired upon the crowd before them, and had killed and wounded several persons. They did not all fire together, as if by the order of an officer, but first one gun was discharged and a man was killed by the bullet—then, after a moment's pause, two more, in quick succession, and then others. There was so much confusion arising from the hootings and hallooings of the mob, and their cries of

"Fire! Fire away! Fire if you dare!" and the hurrying of people to and fro, that it could never be satisfactorily ascertained whether Captain Preston gave the order or not. When the affair was afterward legally investigated, the men declared that Captain Preston ordered them to fire. Several of the bystanders also testified to hearing him give the order, some say that he accompanied it with oaths and imprecations. He himself declared that he did not give any such order. He said that on the contrary, he called out to them, "Don't fire." As, however, it was murder for soldiers to fire upon unarmed men without an order from the officer in command; and not much less than that for any officer to give such an order without being authorized by the civil authority, in a community not under martial law, it became a matter of vital importance on the one hand to the men, to prove that they received the order, and on the other hand to the captain that he did not give it. They were thus all deeply interested witnesses, and people could not tell which to believe.

The bystanders who were present gave the same conflicting testimony. Those whose sympathies were with the government—and several such were near—were sure that Captain Preston did not give the order; while several of the townspeople were equally positive that he did. The result of the trial, which took place long afterward, was the acquittal both of the captain and of most of the men.

It is not improbable that in the noise and confusion which prevailed, the soldiers, maddened by the taunts and hootings of the mob, and by the sticks and snowballs thrown at them, and hearing the cries of "Fire! Why don't you fire!" all around them, were deceived, and imagined or half imagined that in shooting at the men before them they were obeying orders, when they were really acting under the impulse of their own resentment and hate. Indeed, we may well imagine that in the case of a file of soldiers in the situation in which these men were placed—exasperated by a mob of men and boys insulting and almost assaulting them, and standing each with his loaded musket presented to the hated assailants, and his finger on the trigger, the sound of the word "Fire!" coming to them in any way, and from any quarter, in the midst of the confusion, would produce the fatal pull by an almost mechanical impulse too sudden and powerful to be controlled.

105

THE PEOPLE OF THE CUSTOM-HOUSE
IMPLICATED

The reader will recollect that the post of the sentinel who was first attacked by the mob, which was the point at which the firing subsequently took place, was in front of the custom-house. Some of the witnesses afterward testified that two of the shots came from the windows of the custom-house itself, in the second story, which, if it had been established as a fact, would have been a very important one. In connection with this subject, there was a boy, named, singularly enough, Charlotte Bourgate, who gave, in substance, the following testimony in an affidavit.

He said he was an indented apprentice, and that he lived at a certain Mr. Hudson's at the North End. That Mr. Hudson went out early in the evening to go to the custom-house to take a glass of wine there with some friends. That after a time he heard the bells ring and thought it was fire, and went into the street, and went at length to the custom-house, where he knocked at the door, and a young man let him in and locked the door after him.

When he had entered the custom-house, he saw Mr. Hudson and another gentleman come downstairs and go into a room.

"And then"—the rest of his testimony I will give substantially in his own words—"four or five men went upstairs, pulling and hauling me after them, and said, 'My good boy, come.' When I was carried into the chamber, there was but one light in the room, and that in a corner of the chamber, where I saw a tall man loading a gun. I saw two guns in the room. There was a number of gentlemen in the room. After the gun was loaded, the tall man gave it to me and told me to fire, and said he would kill me if I did not. I told him I would not. He, drawing a sword out of his cane, told me if I did not fire it he would run the sword through me. The man putting the gun out of the window, it being a little open, I fired it sideway up the street. The tall man then loaded the gun again. I heard the balls go down. The man then laid it on the window again and told me to fire it. I told him I would not fire again. He told me he would run me through the body if I did not. Upon which I fired again, in the same way up the street.

"After I fired the second gun, I saw my master in the room. He took a gun and pointed it out of the window. I heard the gun go off. Then a tall man came and clapped me on the shoulders, above and below stairs, and said, 'That's my good boy. I'll give you some money tomorrow.' I said, 'I don't want any money.' There being a light in the lower room, and the door being ajar, I saw that it was the tall man that clapped me on the shoulder.

"Then the young man let me out. When I got out of the house, I saw a number of people in the streets, and ran home as fast as I could, and sat up all night in my master's kitchen.

"And further I say that my master licked me the next night for telling about his firing out of the window, and for fear that I should be licked again, I did deny before Justice Quincy all that I had said, for which I am very sorry.

"And further I say not.

his

CHARLOTTE + BOURGATE."

mark.

THE RESULT OF THE TRIALS

On account of young Bourgate's prevarications and contradictions of himself, but little attention seems to have been paid to the charges made against the custom-house people. But Captain Preston and the soldiers were subsequently brought to trial on a charge of murder; and although they were tried by Massachusetts courts and juries, they were all acquitted but two of the soldiers, who were convicted of manslaughter, and were moderately punished. This result was considered as redounding greatly to the credit of the people of the colony, in respect to their fairness and impartiality in all their deliberate acts—but the acquittal of the men did not any the less dispose the people to retain the name for the affair which it had already universally received, and by which it has since always been designated in history—that of the Boston Massacre.

But we must return to the scene of the riot.

SCENE IN THE STREET AFTER THE FIRING

Immediately after the firing of the soldiers, the people that were directly before and around them fell back, their taunts and shouts of derision now suddenly changed to cries of rage and alarm. Some soon came back to take up the dead and wounded, while others rushed on through the streets in a frenzy, calling out to those whom they met to tell them hurriedly what had happened, and urging them to hasten forward into King Street, where, as they said, the soldiers were massacring the inhabitants. The bells soon began to ring more vehemently than ever, and cries of "Fire! Fire! Turn out! Turn out!" filled the streets. Streams of people soon began to pour in from all directions toward the scene of the conflict, and all was tumult and confusion.

In the meantime the military on their part were not idle. Information of what had happened was very speedily communicated to the barracks, and a number of companies of the Twenty-ninth regiment quartered there, were at once put under arms and marched into the street. The whole of the Fourteenth regiment were also put under arms, but were kept in the barracks ready to be marched out if necessary at a moment's notice.

In the street, the troops and the many hundreds of people that had collected, remained for some time face to face, all in a state of extreme excitement and agitation, and each party waiting the arrival of the superior to whom they respectively looked for direction. Captain Preston had sent for Colonel Dalrymple, the commander of the troops, and the people for Hutchinson, acting governor of the colony.

PROCEEDINGS DURING THE NIGHT

These personages, when they arrived upon the spot, entered at once, in connection with the members of the council and other persons of influence in the community, into various negotiations and arrangements with a view to restore quiet. A justice's court was immediately organized, and Captain Preston readily surrendered himself a prisoner, to be tried on any charge which might be brought against him. The soldiers who had fired upon the mob were also delivered up by the military authorities and imprisoned by order of the court. It was decided also that an immediate examination should be made by the court into the circumstances of the event which had occurred, and a guard of one hundred men was organized from among the people to protect the court in its deliberations.

These measures having been taken, the people slowly dispersed, and a comparative degree of quiet for the night was gradually restored.

PROCEEDINGS ON THE FOLLOWING MORNING

It was, however, only the superficial agitation which had been allayed, for the next morning, it was found that the excitement produced by the events of the night was rapidly deepening and extending. Prompt measures were taken to send tidings of what had occurred into the neighboring towns, and by noon large numbers of people were seen coming in all sorts of vehicles into Boston, to give their support and cooperation to any measures which their countrymen might see best to adopt.

MEETING OF THE GOVERNOR AND COUNCIL

Early in the morning a meeting of the governor and council was held, and the selectmen of the town and the justices of the county presented themselves before them with an urgent request that the governor would order the troops to be removed from the town. It would not be possible, they said, to appease the people, while the soldiers remained, and the most direful consequences might result at any moment if their removal was delayed.

Governor Hutchinson was greatly perplexed in this emergency. To order the soldiers to be withdrawn would seem to be compelling the military to retreat before a mob, and this he knew would not only be humiliating to them, but would tend to injure him in the estimation of the government in England—the party in this contest that he chiefly sympathized with, and the one whose favor he was most anxious to retain. On the other hand, he was a Bostonian, and he could not well stand long against the united and most determined will of his countrymen.

Accordingly, in reply to the demand of the selectmen, he said it was not in *his* power to remove the troops. Colonel Dalrymple was the man, and he sent for Colonel Dalrymple.

Colonel Dalrymple said that he should not dare to take the responsibility of removing the troops unless he had an order from the governor to justify him in such a step. He showed, moreover, that unless when there was an officer of a higher rank than he, in command, the troops were at the disposal of the governor of the colony.

This threw the responsibility back upon the governor, and he was perplexed and undecided, and nothing was done.

Meeting of Citizens in Faneuil Hall

In the meantime, a meeting of citizens was called in Faneuil Hall, and at eleven o'clock a very large assembly had convened. The meeting was opened with prayer by Dr. Cooper, the minister of the Brattle Street church, and a man of the very highest standing. The action which was taken by this meeting was the appointment of a committee of fourteen to proceed to the council chamber and to demand, in the name of the people of Boston, the immediate removal of the troops, declaring at the same time that the inhabitants and the soldiery could no longer live together in safety, and that nothing but the immediate removal of the troops could prevent a new outbreak and a general carnage. At the head of this committee was the venerable Samuel Adams, one of the most distinguished and highly respected of the citizens.

The meeting having appointed this committee, and finding that the hall was not large enough to contain the throngs that came both from the town and the country to witness the proceedings, adjourned to the Old South Church, where they were to receive the committee and hear their report.

CONFERENCE WITH THE GOVERNOR

The committee proceeded at once to the council chamber, and there, when they had delivered their message, the governor attempted to argue the case with them, saying that any attack upon the troops by the people would be high treason, and that all engaged in it would forfeit their lives. The committee had no reply to make to this except to repeat their demand that the troops should be removed.

Colonel Dalrymple all the time stood by, declining to take any responsibility in the matter. He was under the governor's orders, he said, and would retain the troops in town, or remove them to the castle, just as his excellency should decide.

Thus forced to come to a decision, the governor concluded to try the effect of a compromise. So he said to the committee that they might report to the people of the town that he would order the Twenty-ninth regiment to be removed to the castle, but the Fourteenth would remain in town, though he would see that effectual measures were adopted to keep them under very close supervision, so that the inhabitants should have nothing to fear from them.

REPORT OF THE COMMITTEE

The committee having received this reply, left the council chamber, which, as the reader will recollect, was in the building still standing at the head of State Street, and proceeded along the street toward the Old South Church. The street was filled with throngs of people, through which the committee walked in solemn procession, with their venerable chairman at the head of it, till they reached the church.

The church was crowded. A passage was, however, soon made for the committee up the thronged aisle, and Mr. Adams made his report. The meeting voted unanimously that the report was unsatisfactory. They immediately appointed a second committee, consisting, like the other, of the very first gentlemen of Boston, in respect to wealth, position and influence, and with Samuel Adams still at the head of it, to proceed again to the council chamber, and renew their demand for the immediate removal of all the troops.

THE DEMAND UPON THE GOVERNOR RENEWED

The new committee, led by their venerable chairman, proceeded at once to the council chamber, and there delivered to the governor their second message. He was more embarrassed and perplexed than ever. He repeated the declaration which he had made before, that he had no power to remove the troops. It was very inconsiderate for him to say this, for he had already promised to remove one of the regiments, and Adams accordingly at once replied that if he had power over one regiment he had power over both. At any rate, the people insisted absolutely that the soldiers should go, and if he refused to order their removal, he must be responsible for the consequences.

Colonel Dalrymple stood by all the time, but gave the governor no help in his perplexity. He was ready to obey an order if the governor would issue one, but he would take no share of the responsibility of removing the troops. On the contrary, he said that the threatening and revolutionary attitude which the people of the town and of the vicinity had assumed was a reason, in his opinion, why they should *not* be removed.

The council, on the other hand, after due deliberation, were unanimous in advising that the governor should give the order, and the governor finally decided to comply. Colonel Dalrymple on receiving it said that he should obey it, and promised to take the troops away without any unnecessary delay.

The committee then returned to the meeting at the Old South Church, to report the successful result of their mission, and the meeting adjourned. A large militia force was, however, at once raised to watch over the safety of the town and of the inhabitants while the troops remained.

These measures having been taken, a certain degree of quiet was gradually restored to the town, and preparations began to be made for the interment of the victims of the massacre. The funerals, some of which were from the homes of the deceased, and others from Faneuil Hall, were celebrated with great parade, and were attended by an immense concourse of citizens. The new guards were posted in the streets. The soldiers were kept confined in their barracks, where they muttered their vain rage and resentment at the humiliating position they occupied—two British regiments held thus as it were prisoners, by the citizens of a miserable provincial town.

Both they and their officers were extremely reluctant to go away, and in order to soften the mortification of their defeat, the officers seemed to take as much time as possible in making the necessary preparations. A fortnight elapsed before they were ready to go, but they were then finally embarked in boats and taken down to the castle, on one of the islands of the harbor.

Thus the affair, so far as relates to the immediate action of the parties concerned, was ended; but as the tidings of it spread through the country and passed across the ocean to the government in London, the effects which it produced were of vast importance. In America, it greatly extended and strengthened the growing feeling of disaffection toward the government of the mother country, and in England it produced a feeling of exasperation in the ministry, which made them more ready than ever to adopt the severest measures against the refractory colonists. They felt that a body of British troops had been ignominiously hustled out by a mob from the post where the government had deliberately placed them, and thus that the military power of the British empire had been insulted and defied by a set of vulgar merchants and citizens, the despised population of a provincial town. Such a rebuff was of course not to be submitted to. The difficulty was to determine in what way the stinging injury should be redressed and avenged.

CHAPTER VIII
POPULAR OUTBREAKS

Long Protraction of the Preliminary Contest

The affair of the Boston Massacre, so called, occurred in the year 1770, five years before the war between the colonial government and the mother country was commenced by the battle of Lexington, which took place in the same month of April, in 1775. Thus, the preliminary contests which preceded the actual commencement of hostilities between the colonies and the mother country were protracted through a series of several years.

Excitement in England Produced by the Boston Massacre

The news of the firing upon the people of Boston by the troops, and of the consequent somewhat ignominious expulsion of the military from the town, awakened a great excitement in England. The intelligence produced a double effect. It aroused the government to a feeling of resentment, and to a determination to bring the refractory colonists to due submission by some means or other, at all hazards. On the other hand, it awakened the friends of the colonists, and all those who had been opposed to the policy of governing them with a strong hand, which the ministry had now been pursuing for several years, to make fresh efforts to have this policy reversed, in order that the disastrous consequences which they anticipated from the continuance of it might be averted.

Resolutions Offered in the House of Commons

The last named party accordingly brought forward resolutions in the House of Commons recommending the total repeal of all the measures which had been adopted for the past ten years for taxing and coercing the colonies, and restoring everything to the state existing at the commencement of the reign.

In the course of the debate on these resolutions, the party advocating them showed how completely the ministry had failed in all their plans.

"You have imposed taxes," said they, "and then repealed them again. You have attempted to raise a revenue in America for the purpose of relieving somewhat the burdens of the people of England, but have thereby only produced an aggravation of the distress of the British merchants and manufacturers. You have formed schemes which you said were to fortify and strengthen the British dominion in America, and they have issued in a state of things which threaten its entire overthrow. You have dissolved assemblies in America for contumacy, and then allowed them to be reconvoked without their having made the slightest concession. You have denounced multitudes of the colonists as guilty of sedition, and even of treason, without having been able to bring a single individual to trial and punishment. You have sent troops to prevent a rebellion, and their presence and action only served to provoke one. And now, in the end, every branch of the British government in America is seen to be degraded, and the resentment and resistance of the colonists is continually increasing and extending, and is everywhere triumphant."

This state of things, they urged, proved conclusively that the course of policy which had produced it ought to be at once totally abandoned.

THE MINISTRY WILL NOT YIELD

These arguments, though entirely unanswerable, were not calculated to have much effect in inducing the ministry to yield. On the contrary, their wounded pride received only a fresh exasperation from them, and they exerted all the political influence which they could bring to bear upon the House of Commons, to procure votes against the resolutions. The resolutions were consequently defeated, and the government were accordingly allowed to persevere.

Rigorous Measures Adopted

One of the immediate effects which was produced in England by the refractory and rebellious spirit, as they termed it, that the colonists displayed, was to cause orders to be given to the governors of the different provinces, the collectors of the customs, and other officers, to be more strict and stringent than ever in carrying the laws into execution, and in exacting the fees, the duties and the other payments of various kinds which it devolved upon them to collect; and also to enforce in the most rigid manner the regulations and restrictions in respect to foreign commerce which were in force under existing laws. There resulted from this increased pressure, and also from the domineering and haughty manner in which the officials performed these duties, a great deal of dissatisfaction and resentment on the part of the people, which led to several serious outbreaks some time before the commencement of open war. Some of these outbreaks occurred before, and some after the affair of the massacre.

The North Carolina Regulators

One of the most serious of these outbreaks was that of the regulators, so called, of North Carolina. It seems that the people of that colony became at last so incensed at the various impositions and abuses practiced upon them by the officers of the government, in charging exorbitant fees for legal documents and proceedings, and collecting taxes in a vexatious and extortionate manner, that at length a large number of the poorer classes banded themselves together and took a solemn pledge not to pay any taxes at all until these abuses were corrected, and the fees and charges which they complained of were regulated in some just and equitable manner. The people thus combined were called *regulators*.

The Party of the Regulators Increased and Strengthened

The party of the regulators, after increasing slowly for a time, received at length a great impulse and extension by certain acts of the government which the common people thought outrageous. For these acts, however, it was quite as much upon their own colonial government itself, as upon the authority of the crown that the responsibility fell; and thus the rebellion of the regulators was never exactly considered as an incident of the revolt of the colonies against the mother country.

One of the things which greatly displeased the poorer class of taxpayers, was a vote of the assembly to build a palace for the governor, as an expression of public gratitude for the repeal of the Stamp Act. The people were the more incensed at this as it happened that the period for beginning to collect the tax assessed for the purpose of building this palace, came just at the time that the new tax which Parliament had laid on the five necessary articles of consumption—glass, lead, paper, paints and tea—was promulgated. It seemed very hard to the poor backwoodsmen that they should be compelled to contribute from their scanty earnings to build a palace for a governor in thanks for the repeal of an odious law which was immediately replaced by one still more odious.

In another instance, one of the public officers was accused of extortion and brought to trial on six indictments, and found guilty in every instance. But the royal judges only sentenced him to pay a fine of one penny.

FEW—THE LEADER OF THE REGULATORS

These occurrences greatly increased the exasperation of the people, and added to the number of the regulators, who at length banded themselves together under the leadership of a poor and ignorant man like themselves, named Few. After a time they assembled to the number of two thousand and declared for a revolution. Few announced that he was commissioned from heaven to free the world from oppression, beginning with North Carolina, where he and his followers were first to abolish all courts of justice, exterminate all lawyers and public officers, overturn the provincial government, and establish an entirely new political dispensation founded on the principles of justice and the rights of man.

Defeat of the Regulators

Of course, all the better portion of the people of the colony were ready to sustain any measures necessary for putting down such a movement as this. The governor organized a military force and went out to attack the regulators in their camp, which was upon the river Allamance, in the interior and toward the northern part of the colony.

When the governor approached the place where the regulators were assembled, he sent forward a summons to them to lay down their arms and surrender. They refused to do it, and prepared to defend themselves to the best of their ability. The governor then ordered the troops to advance with the artillery, and the battle commenced. It was short and decisive. The insurgents could not stand against the troops. Their scanty supply of ammunition was soon exhausted. Twenty or thirty of them were killed or wounded. The rest dispersed. Few himself was taken prisoner, and the next day was hung upon a tree, as an outlaw.

The governor then proceeded to scour the country with his troops, laying waste the farms and destroying the property of the poor regulators, and offering rewards for the apprehension of the leaders. Many of them were taken and were executed in a very summary manner. Of the rest, some perished miserably, while numbers escaped into neighboring colonies, and some crossed the mountains to the westward, and there commenced life anew by founding settlements in the wilderness, among the Indians and bears.

The Sloop *Liberty*

The most frequent difficulties, however, in these times occurred in the towns on the seaboard, where the laws in respect to duties on imports were to be executed by revenue vessels and custom-house officers. One case that for a time produced much excitement was that of the sloop *Liberty*.

The sloop *Liberty* was an armed revenue cutter, that was fitted out in Boston by the government officers there and sent to Rhode Island under the command of a certain Captain Reid, to enforce the revenue laws at the harbor of Newport. Captain Reid proceeded to his station, and began to execute his commission, acting, as the colonists thought, in a very arbitrary and imperious manner.

Among other things, he seized and brought into port two vessels belonging to Connecticut. While the vessels were lying in the port, in possession of Captain Reid, under the charge of having violated the revenue laws in some way, Captain Packwood, the captain of one of them, accompanied by two of his men, went on board his vessel, which was at anchor at a little distance from the shore, in order to obtain some of his wearing apparel; but was told when he got on board, that his effects had all been sent on board his majesty's sloop *Liberty*.

Captain Packwood then asked for his sword, and he was told that a man belonging to the *Liberty*, who with others had been put on board the vessel to hold it in charge, was lying upon the locker which contained it, in the cabin.

He accordingly went below in search of his sword, and was received there by the man in charge in a very rough manner, and ordered off with oaths and imprecations. Captain Packwood attempted to obtain his sword, and a struggle ensued between him and his men on the one side, and the men of the *Liberty* on the other. He succeeded at length in getting possession or the sword, and then he and the two men who had come with him rushed to the deck, got into their boat and pushed off toward the shore, taking the prize with them.

The officer from the *Liberty*, who had followed the men to the deck, ordered his men to fire upon them as they rowed away, and three shots were fired, one from a musket and two from a pair of pistols.

Resentment of the People

No one was hurt by the firing, but the people of the town were made so indignant by the act, that a large body of them met and intercepted Captain Reid on the following evening, upon the wharf; and demanded that the man who had fired upon Captain Packwood should be sent on shore and delivered up to the authorities.

Captain Reid was somewhat intimidated by the numbers and excitement of the people, and ho promised to comply. He sent out to the sloop and a man was brought on shore. He had selected, on purpose probably, the wrong man.

Captain Packwood declared that this was not the guilty person, and Captain Reid sent for another, and then another, until nearly all the crew were on shore. The crowd on the wharf then immediately made a rush to the boats and went off to the sloop, and at once proceeded to cut away her cables and set her adrift.

The vessel floated over across the harbor and grounded there upon a shoal. Here the men cut away her mast, threw overboard her armament and stores of war, scuttled her, and then left her to the mercy of the winds and waves.

They took the boats as trophies of their victory back to the town, and when they landed, they attached ropes to them, and dragged them in triumph through the streets. It is said that the keels of the boats were shod with iron, and that so large was the force of men that manned the ropes, and so great the speed at which they raced through the streets with them, that the friction of the keels upon the pavement left a long stream of fire behind them as they were swept along.

The abandoned vessel remained where she had been left, for some days, and then one evening, just after a severe thundershower, she was discovered to be on fire. She continued to burn for several days until almost entirely consumed.

This affair of the sloop *Liberty* is said to have been the first instance in which there was a direct attack by any of the people of America upon any authorized and official representative of the sovereign power of Britain, and was thus, as it were, the first overt act of the rebellion. There had been many riots and disturbances, and some acts of violence before; but they had been directed against private persons, or at least against persons not at the time in the exercise of military or official power. Here, however, was an armed vessel, in the actual service of his majesty, attacked by a mob, captured and destroyed.

THE AFFAIR OF THE *GASPEE*

Serious as this affair was, another somewhat analogous to it, but much more serious, occurred in nearly the same place, in the spring of 1772, and which is known as the affair of the *Gaspee*.

The *Gaspee* was a schooner armed with eight guns, that was stationed in Narragansett Bay, in company with another vessel named the *Beaver,* to enforce the revenue laws. Lieutenant Duddingston was the officer in command of her. The people complained that he executed the duties of his office in a very arbitrary and vexatious manner. They said that he practiced every possible annoyance upon vessels in the bay, detaining them often unnecessarily, and when he had no reason whatever to suspect anything wrong. He even stopped the market-boats which came from the landings along the bay with farm and garden produce for the town. He made seizures when he had no right to do so, and sent the seized vessels sometimes to Boston to be tried, which was contrary to law.

INEFFECTUAL ATTEMPTS TO PROCURE REDRESS

These complaints became at length so numerous and so urgent that the attention of the government of the colony was called to them, and in the end the governor sent a communication to Lieutenant Duddingston, by the hands of the high sheriff, and a long negotiation ensued, which resulted very unsatisfactorily. The lieutenant resented and resisted the governor's attempt to call him to account and to hold him amenable to law, and he appealed to Admiral Montagu, the officer in command at Boston, who sustained him fully in the position he had taken, and wrote in very imperious terms to the governor, declaring that the officers in command of the revenue vessels on the coast would continue the course they had been pursuing, and that if the people of the colony attempted any open resistance, he would hang them as pirates.

THE *GASPEE* RUNS AGROUND

Things were in this state, when one day a vessel named the *Hannah,* commanded by Captain Lindsey, in coming from New York to Providence, touched at Newport, and was going on the next day up the bay, when the *Gaspee* hailed her, and attempted to bring her to. The *Hannah,* however, passed on, and the *Gaspee* gave chase, but in passing a certain point which, from this circumstance has since been known as Gaspee Point, she ran aground. The *Hannah* went on and reached Providence in safety, and immediately Captain Lindsey gave notice there of the dangerous situation that the *Gaspee* was in. The result was that that night a boat expedition was fitted out from Providence to go down the river and destroy her.

JOHN BROWN

The man who took the lead in this first open attempt to organize a military resistance to the power which was threatening to overwhelm the liberties of the country, was named John Brown. He was one of the first and most respectable merchants of Providence. Captain Lindsey, knowing probably his sentiments and his character, went immediately on his arrival to his counting room, and made known to him the fact that the *Gaspee* was aground about seven miles below, and that on account of the falling tide she could not get off until after midnight.

PREPARATIONS FOR AN ATTACK ON THE *GASPEE*

Mr. Brown immediately resolved upon the destruction of the vessel, and he at once charged one of the shipmasters in his employ to collect eight of the largest longboats in the harbor, with five oars to each, to have the oars and rowlocks muffled to prevent noise, and to place them all at a wharf opposite a certain house of entertainment kept by Mr. Sabin, where the party that was intended to man the boats could conveniently assemble.

Having caused these preparations to be made, Mr. Brown waited until after sunset, and then sent a man about the streets nearest to the shipping to beat a drum, and to inform the people whose attention should be arrested by the drum, that the *Gaspee* was aground about seven miles below, and to invite all persons who were disposed to join an expedition for going down and destroying her, to repair at nine o'clock to the house of entertainment above referred to.

Account Given by One of the Participants in the Affair

I will relate the story of the manner in which the party thus organized carried Mr. Brown's plan into effect, in the words substantially of Ephraim Powen, one of the men who was present and took part in the affair.

"About nine o'clock I took my father's gun and my powder horn and bullets, and went to Mr. Sabin's, and found the southeast room full of people. Here I loaded my gun and we all remained here until about ten o'clock—some casting bullets in the kitchen, and others making arrangements for departure—when orders were given to cross the street to Fenner's Wharf and embark.

"This we soon did. We had a sea captain on board each boat to act as steersman, of whom I recollect Captain Abraham Whipple, Captain John B. Hopkins, who steered the boat that I was in, and Captain Benjamin Dunn. A line was formed by the boats from right to left, with Captain Whipple on the right.

"The boats proceeded in this order down the bay, and went on until some time past midnight they reached within about sixty yards of the *Gaspee,* when a sentinel on board hailed,

"'Who comes there?'

"No answer.

"He hailed again and no answer. In about a minute Duddingston was seen mounted on the starboard gunwale in his night dress, and hailed,

"'Who comes there?'

"No answer.

"He hailed again, when at length Captain Whipple called out, with a great oath,

"'I am the sheriff of the county of Kent. I have got a warrant to apprehend you, so surrender.'

"I took my seat upon the main thwart, near the larboard rowlock facing forwards, and with my gun by my right side. As soon as Duddingston began to hail, Joseph Bucklin, who was standing on the main thwart, by my right side, said to me,

"'Ephraim, reach me up your gun. I can kill that fellow.'

"I reached it to him accordingly and then, just as Captain Whipple was replying and calling upon him to surrender, Bucklin fired and Duddingston fell; upon which Bucklin exclaimed,

"'I have killed the rascal.'

"In less than a minute after this the boats were alongside the *Gaspee,* and she was boarded without opposition. The men on deck retreated below as we came up, and Duddingston was led into the cabin. As soon as we found that he was wounded, one of our men, John Mawney, who had been studying physic and surgery for two or three years, was ordered to go below and dress his wound, and I was directed to go and assist him.

"On the examination, it was found that the ball took effect about five inches directly below the navel. Duddingston called for Mr. Dickinson to produce bandages and other necessaries for dressing the wound, and when this was done orders were given to the schooner's company to collect their clothing and everything belonging to them, and put them into their boats, as all of them were to be sent on shore. All were soon collected and put on board the boats, including one of our own, and were landed at a wharf in Pawtuxet.

"Soon after this all our party went away in the boats, leaving one boat for the leaders of the expedition who, remaining, soon set the vessel on fire, and she was burned to the water's edge."

The foregoing account was written by Mr. Bowen in 1839, sixty-seven years after the occurrence of the affair. Mr. Bowen was at this time eighty-six years of age, by which it appears that at the time of his taking part in the expedition he was at the age of nineteen.

Burning of the Gaspee.

GREAT EXCITEMENT PRODUCED BY THE AFFAIR

Of course so high-handed a measure as the seizing by force of an armed government vessel, accompanied by the wounding of the commanding officer, the dispersion of the crew, and the destruction of the vessel itself and of everything on board, by a company of private persons, acting without the least color of authority, produced a great and universal excitement. The news of it was received almost everywhere among the colonists with feelings of exultation and triumph; while among all the British officials, high and low, it awakened the utmost astonishment and indignation. Duddingston, whose wound proved to be not very severe, caused a statement of what had occurred to be sent to the admiral at Boston who had command of all the naval force on the coast. He immediately sent an urgent and indignant complaint to the governor of Rhode Island, calling upon him to take the most vigorous measures for discovering the guilty persons, and for bringing them to immediate punishment. The governor, after some negotiations with the admiral, and consultations with his council, concluded to offer a reward of a sum equal to five hundred dollars for the discovery of the guilty persons. But nobody came forward to give their testimony.

ROYAL COMMISSION APPOINTED

When the news of the occurrence reached England, the ministry issued what is called a royal commission—that is, a special authority granted to a select body of men, to investigate the affair, and, if possible, to bring the guilty parties to justice. The commissioners appointed were invested with extraordinary powers, and they consisted of some of the most prominent men in America, that were supposed to be in sympathy with the home government, such as governors, and judges of the higher courts in the different colonies. The commission itself, authenticated by the royal signature and seal, was sent out to the admiral, and he communicated it to the governor of Rhode Island who notified the persons appointed. Their orders were if they could obtain probable evidence against any persons, implicating them in the transaction, to report their names to the governor of Rhode Island who was to arrest the persons thus charged, and send them as prisoners to England for trial.

The commissioners met and commenced the work of investigation, which they continued at intervals for several months; but in the end they came to the conclusion to send a report to his majesty, under whose direct authority they had been appointed and were acting, that they had failed to make any material discovery, and that they believed that the whole affair was conducted so secretly and suddenly, as to make it now nearly impossible to ascertain who the guilty persons were.

AARON BRIGGS

The only important evidence that was brought forward before the commissioners during these investigations, was that of a mulatto man, a slave, named Aaron Briggs. He was engaged in the expedition, and he afterward ran away from his master and escaped on board the *Beaver*, the consort, as perhaps the reader will recollect, of the *Gaspee*, in guarding the harbor. Here he told the story more or less correctly to the sailors on board, and the captain of the *Beaver* hearing of his revelations, examined him, and finally compelled him to make an affidavit in respect to the persons engaged, and then sent the affidavit to the governor of Rhode Island, with a request that he would cause the persons therein named to be arrested.

But instead of doing this the governor, after proper consultation and enquiry, obtained a number of affidavits from respectable persons in Providence who testified that Aaron Briggs was an unprincipled fellow notoriously unworthy of belief in respect to any statements that he might make; and these affidavits he sent to the admiral, saying that he did not feel justified in arresting any persons on the unsupported testimony of such a man.

The affidavit of the mulatto was afterward brought before the commissioners, and they, after a full hearing, decided that independently of the character of the deponent, there was proof that the affidavit was *extorted* from him by the captain of the *Beaver*, and was of course not to be received.

Except this poor slave, not one of all the hundreds in Providence who must have known the parties concerned in the affair, came forward to give testimony—although in addition to the reward offered by the governor, other rewards were offered in other ways amounting in all to some thousands of dollars.

ABRAHAM WHIPPLE

In connection with this subject, an anecdote has been preserved relating to Captain Abraham Whipple, who, it will be recollected, was the leader of the expedition of the boats, being put in command of it by John Brown, the merchant with whom the plan originated, and who made the arrangements, and provided the means for executing it. Sometime after this, when the war of the revolution broke out, this same Captain Whipple commanded a war sloop belonging to Rhode Island, which was engaged in hostilities with a frigate called the *Rose,* under the command of Captain Wallace. Captain Wallace, it seems, had learned that Captain Whipple had been a leader in the capture of the *Gaspee.* In the course of the operations in which they were engaged, it is said that the following correspondence took place.

Captain Wallace wrote first, as follows:

"You, Abraham Whipple, on the 10th of June, 1772, burned his majesty's vessel the *Gaspee,* and I will hang you at the yard-arm."

Captain Whipple sent the following reply.

"To SIR JAMES WALLACE ,
"SIR,—Always catch a man before you hang him.
"ABRAHAM WHIPPLE."

Captain Whipple was very soon after this placed in command, as commodore, of two vessels of war armed and equipped for the defense of Rhode Island. They were called the *Washington* and the *Katy.* This unpretending squadron was the commencement of the American navy.

The fitting out of this little squadron, however, and the connection of Captain Whipple with it, are stated here in anticipation, as these things did not take place until the breaking out of the revolution in 1775, two or three years after the destruction of the *Gaspee*.

THE BOSTON TEA PARTY

The next popular outbreak of sufficient importance to attract general attention was the one known in history as the destruction of the tea in Boston harbor—though the affair is often designated as the Boston Tea Party. The exploit, for some reason or other, produced a more widely extended and more continued excitement than the destruction of the *Gaspee;* although the latter really required a far higher degree of resolution and daring on the part of the men engaged in it. The circumstances which led to the destruction of the tea were these.

INGENIOUS CONTRIVANCE OF THE BRITISH GOVERNMENT FOR INDUCING THE COLONIES TO SUBMIT TO BE TAXED

The reader will recollect, perhaps, that on account of the decided attitude of resistance to the policy of the mother country, which the colonies were assuming, and the frequent disturbances and difficulties which began to arise, the government repealed the duties on the five articles of glass, lead, paints, paper and tea excepting those on the last, and that this duty they made very small. Their policy was to reduce the actual amount of the taxation to so small a measure as to make it practically insignificant, while yet in theory it sustained the principle. They imagined that by this plan they could so weaken the opposition to their measures that they could go on with the small impost for a while, till the excitement had passed away, and everything had become quiet, when they could gradually increase and extend the taxation again, slowly, cautiously, and perhaps covertly, and so avoid awakening the opposition a second time.

THE PLAN DOES NOT SUCCEED

But the Americans understood this policy as well as they did, and set themselves at work resolutely to resist it, by forming combinations against the purchase of tea, and even against allowing any merchants to import it or to keep it for sale, and by other similar measures. These measures were so successful that the market for tea in America was almost entirely cut off from the English merchants of the East India Company, by whom the tea was imported from China. The company, however, supposing as they did that this interruption to the trade would be only temporary, continued to import tea, and the result was, after the lapse of some months, that the article began to accumulate in enormous quantities in their vast warehouses in London, and the merchants found themselves greatly straightened and distressed.

ANOTHER VERY INGENIOUS SCHEME ADOPTED

The government now fell upon another very ingenious scheme for surmounting the difficulty in which they and the East India Company were alike involved, which was to remit the *export* duty on the tea. According to the law as it then stood, the tea was subject to a large duty, when it was taken from the warehouses of the company to be exported to foreign countries. This duty the company of course added to the price which they charged for the tea, and this addition considerably enhanced the cost to the foreign consumer. The government now conceived the idea of *remitting* for a time this duty, while they still retained the American tax. The remitting of the export duty would so reduce the price in America, that the Americans could pay the small tax required of them, and yet purchase their tea cheaper than ever before, which circumstance they thought would disarm the opposition entirely. The friends of the government in America would say to the people, "How senseless it is in you to deprive yourselves of what has become one of the great necessaries of life for you, on account of a petty nominal tax, when the tax is accompanied by another measure which makes your tea cost you less than it ever did before!"

Accordingly the company immediately shipped a large quantity of tea to the different ports in America—to Boston, to New York, to Philadelphia, and to Charleston.

Disposition Made of the Tea Sent to the More Southern Ports

When the ship sent to Charleston arrived, the people had a meeting and took the cargo of tea under their own charge. They allowed it to be landed, but required it to be stored in a place by itself, where a strong guard was set over it. Either by accident or design the place selected was damp, and the tea was kept in it until it was totally spoiled.

In New York and Philadelphia the persons to whom the tea was consigned, were compelled to refuse to receive it, and it was accordingly sent back to England.

The Boston Consignees Called upon to Resign

The merchants in Boston to whom the cargoes destined for that port were consigned, were not so manageable. They could not be induced to refuse to receive the tea. Various public and private meetings of citizens were held, and at length one morning in November, just before day, a violent knocking was heard at the doors of the consignees, and on going to the door the several parties received a notification summoning them to appear the next day at noon, under the Liberty Tree; and there publicly to resign their commissions.

At the same time there were posted placards throughout the town, containing the following notification.

"To the Freemen of this and the Neighboring Towns.

"Gentlemen,
"You are desired to meet at the Liberty Tree this day at twelve o'clock at noon, then and there to hear the persons to whom the tea shipped by the East India Company is consigned, make a public resignation of their office as consignees, upon oath—and also swear that they will reship any teas that may be consigned to them by the said company by the first vessel sailing for London.

"0. C., Secretary.

"Boston, Nov. 3d, 1773.

"☞Show us the men who will dare take this notice down."

THE MEETING AT THE LIBERTY TREE

Early in the morning a large flag was hung out from the pole at the tree. The bells rang for an hour before the time of the meeting, and the town crier went through the streets calling upon the people to assemble. About five hundred persons came together—but the consignees did not appear.

SUBSEQUENT PROCEEDINGS

It was rumored at the meeting that the consignees were all assembled at a store in King Street belonging to one of the principal tea-importing firms, and the meeting appointed a committee to proceed there and wait upon them, and ascertain what they intended to do. The meeting also resolved to accompany this committee in mass, partly from the impatience of the people to know the result, and partly to make their demonstration the more imposing.

The committee were received by the consignees at the store, and some negotiations took place, but without leading to anything satisfactory. The people became very much excited, but they were at length in some degree quieted, and induced to disperse without doing any serious damage.

TOWN MEETING CALLED

The next day a regular town meeting was held. There, after some earnest debate, most decided resolutions were adopted against submitting to the proposed tax, and another committee was appointed to wait upon the consignees, and to make a fresh demand upon them in the name of the town.

The meeting then adjourned to the afternoon to give the committee an opportunity to perform the duty assigned them.

At the re-assembling of the meeting in the afternoon the committee reported that they had conferred with the consignees, but could not induce them to refuse receiving the tea. On the contrary they sent in replies to the demand which had been made upon them, which were voted by the meeting to be "daringly affrontive to the town."

INCREASE OF EXCITEMENT

Of course these proceedings, and the failure of the efforts made to induce the consignees to yield greatly increased the excitement. The tea had not yet arrived, but the coming of the vessels into the harbor might be expected at any time; and during the interval the agitation of the people of the town, and the preparations for adopting decisive measures against the consignees, seemed daily to increase.

EVENING PARTY AT THE HOUSE OF A CONSIGNEE

There was a certain mercantile firm—the Messrs. Clarke, whose feelings and sympathies, it seems, were strongly on the British side, and who had taken special pains to have a portion of the tea consigned to them, and they had some time previously sent out a young man to England—one of their clerks—to make application to the company for it. This young man now returned, having successfully accomplished his mission. A voyage to Europe in those days was a much more serious affair than it is now, and when their clerk arrived, one of the firm, who lived in a handsome house in School Street, gave a party in honor of his safe return from so long a voyage, after having successfully accomplished his enterprise.

In the evening, while the party thus assembled were in the midst of their hilarity and enjoyment, there suddenly appeared in the street, before the house, a mob of wild and excited men, who began to thump upon the door, and to create all possible disturbance by whistling, shouting, blowing of horns, uttering cat-calls, and making every conceivable outlandish noise. They crowded into the yard and up to the windows of the house, and seemed on the eve of actually assaulting the building and carrying it by storm.

The ladies were of course greatly frightened. They were immediately all conveyed away from the front rooms by the gentlemen, and hid in dark closets and obscure passages. One of the gentlemen then went up to the story above and opening the window there, he warned the rioters to disperse. They replied by throwing stones at him. He then discharged a pistol over their heads, which only increased the tumult, and for a few minutes the affair threatened to become very serious.

But some well-disposed person of the town, in whom the leaders of the mob seemed to have confidence, soon appeared, and after a while succeeded, though with great difficulty and after much delay, in inducing the people to disperse.

Flight of the Consignees from the Town

The consignees now began to feel seriously alarmed, but they were still determined not to yield to the pressure. So they made a formal appeal to the governor and council for protection. The excitement still continued and grew daily more and more threatening, and a day or two after they had made their appeal to the governor, they all suddenly disappeared from the town, and it was soon ascertained that they had gone to the castle for safety.

Arrival of the First Cargo of Tea

At length, on Sunday, November 28th, the *Dartmouth,* the ship containing the first consignment of tea, arrived in the harbor. The news produced intense excitement throughout the town. The people would not call a public meeting on the Sabbath, but the selectmen came together to adopt some preliminary measures. They attempted to obtain an interview with the consignees, but they were not to be found. As has already been stated, they had sought refuge at the castle.

Measures were then immediately taken for calling a meeting of the people on the following day. Accordingly, early on Monday morning, bills were found posted everywhere along the streets; calling upon the people to assemble in Faneuil Hall at nine o'clock, at which time the bells would be rung to give notice. At the appointed time a very large number of persons came together.

Public Meeting on Monday

The proceedings were commenced by the bringing forward of a resolution that the tea which had arrived in the harbor should be sent back whence it came, at all hazards. This resolution was passed, but as it was found that the hall was not large enough to contain the multitudes that were crowding to the meeting, not only from Boston itself, but from all the surrounding towns, it was voted to adjourn to the Old South Church—or rather to the South Meeting-house. for that was the name by which the edifice was then known.

Faneuil Hall, which has since been greatly enlarged, so that now it will contain an immense assemblage, was then a building of moderate size, being intended only for the accommodation of the ordinary town meetings.

The proceedings which had been commenced at the hall were continued at the meeting-house, and resolutions were passed demanding in the most decided manner of the consignees that they should send the tea immediately back to England, and that, too, without paying any duty upon it whatever in the port of Boston.

The meeting then adjourned to the afternoon, in order to give time to the consignees to return their answer.

In the afternoon, the consignees sent a message by a friend that they could not give their answer until the next day, and asked indulgence of the meeting for the delay.

The meeting voted to grant the delay asked for, and resolved to adjourn until the next morning at nine o'clock.

The assembly, however, before adjourning, voted to send a peremptory order to Captain Hall, the master of the ship containing the tea, requiring him not to land the tea, saying that if he did so it would be at his peril. A watch also was appointed of twenty-five persons to keep guard by night on the wharf, to prevent the secret landing of the tea under cover of darkness.

Meeting on Tuesday

On Tuesday the meeting was again convened to hear the answer of the consignees. Their answer was that on looking into their instructions from the East India Company, they found that they had no authority to send back the tea; but they were willing to land and store it, and not offer it for sale until they could write to the company and receive further orders from them.

Proclamation from the Governor

Of course this answer was entirely unsatisfactory, and immediately after it was received, a person appeared in the meeting, saying that he had in his hand a proclamation from the governor. He was the sheriff. A vote was passed giving him permission to read the proclamation. The purport of it proved to be a denunciation of the meeting as a lawless and riotous assembly, and an order for the persons composing it immediately to disperse.

This summons was received with hisses and derisive laughter, and after it was read, the meeting proceeded with the transaction of the business before it, without paying any regard to the momentary interruption.

Definite Measures Adopted

The measures adopted at this and the preceding meetings were these:

First, the issuing of a peremptory order to the owner of the ship, who was a Boston merchant—a member of the Society of Friends, named Rotch—forbidding him to discharge the rest of his cargo, but requiring him to retain the tea on board and to carry it back to England, on the return voyage of the vessel. The time allowed him for doing this was twenty days. The reason for this particular limit will be explained in the sequel.

Secondly, the institution of a watch of twenty-five persons to keep guard every night at Griffin's Wharf, where the ship containing the tea lay, to prevent its being landed clandestinely. If this watch should be in any way interfered with or molested in the night, the alarm was to be given and the bells rung, that the people might assemble to protect them.

Thirdly, the organization of a regular system of communication with the interior towns of the province through a Committee of Correspondence, consisting of a number of the most prominent and influential men in Boston, appointed for the purpose. This committee were to correspond with similar committees, that had been or were to be appointed in all the neighboring towns, so as to be ready to act in concert with them in any sudden emergency. And in the meantime they were to carry into effect the measures which the people had resolved upon.

Six persons were appointed as post-riders to carry the communications of the committee to and fro, and especially to be ready at a moment's notice to ride to all the neighboring towns to give the alarm, in case of any attempt being made to interfere with the watch, or to land the tea.

A Fortnight of Suspense and Negotiation

These measures having been taken, the meeting adjourned, leaving the whole business in the hands of the committee of correspondence until the twenty days allowed to Mr. Rotch for discharging the rest of his cargo and proceeding to sea with the tea should have expired. About a fortnight of this allotted period still remained. During this time two other consignments of tea arrived, in two other vessels—the *Eleanor,* commanded by Captain Bruce, and the *Beaver,* by Captain Coffin. The coming in of these vessels renewed in some measure the excitement in town, but the committee of correspondence immediately gave directions to the masters and owners of them to cause them to be brought to Griffin's Wharf, where the *Dartmouth* was lying, in order that all the cargoes could be watched by the same guard.

The guard, in addition to a strong force at the wharf, stationed armed sentinels all over the town, who called out the time every half hour during the night, like military sentinels on duty, thus:

"Half past twelve o'clock, and all's well!"

These solemn calls, heard all through the night, tended greatly to impress the people with a sense of the momentous character of the crisis, and to extend and deepen the prevailing excitement.

The days passed on, and everyone waited with intense anxiety to know whether the tea would be sent away within the allotted time. During all this time a great many negotiations were taking place among the various parties concerned, which only seemed, however, to involve the affair in greater and greater intricacy and complication.

DIFFICULTIES AND COMPLICATIONS OF THE AFFAIR

It might seem at first view that the question of sending the tea back to England again was a very simple one, and could have been very easily decided in one way or the other; but in fact, the circumstances connected with the case made it really very complicated. To take the case of the *Dartmouth,* for example. The ship belonged to Mr. Rotch, whose only interest was to get rid of the tea in some way or other, and so recover the undisturbed possession of his vessel. He was desirous of landing the tea, but the watch set upon the wharf would not allow him to land it. He then expressed his willingness to take the tea back to London, on his next voyage; but the custom-house authorities declared that they would not give him what is called a clearance—that is, a written certificate that all the requisitions of the custom-house had been complied with—until the tea was landed, and without such a clearance, no vessel was permitted to go to sea. Anyone attempting it would be stopped by the guns of the castle.

If he were to attempt to slip by the castle in the night, or in a fog, without a clearance, then his ship could not enter any foreign port, but was liable to be seized and forfeited wherever found.

Besides, Admiral Montagu, who, as perhaps the reader will recollect, commanded the naval force on the coast, anticipating an attempt on the part of the Bostonians to get the ship to sea with the tea on board, stationed two armed vessels at the mouth of the harbor to intercept and perhaps sink her if she made the attempt. The guns of the castle too were loaded, and strict orders given to watch closely and not allow the vessel to pass.

In the meantime, if the owner failed to perform the duties required of him by the custom-house rules, among which were the obligation to land all his cargo and pay the duties on it, within twenty days after its arrival, his ship was liable to be seized and forfeited, for violation of the revenue laws.

Thus the time given him as his limit, on the one hand, by the custom-house officers for discharging his cargo, and on the other, by the committee of correspondence for taking it to sea again was the same, and as this limit drew near its close, Mr. Rotch found himself in a situation of the greatest perplexity and distress. The guard on the wharf would not allow him to discharge the tea, and the custom-house authorities would not allow him to go to sea with it on board; and if he remained with it where he was for a few days more, the vessel would be seized and confiscated and he would be ruined.

It was the same with the owners of the other two vessels, only as their vessels came in later than the *Dartmouth*, their twenty days would not expire so soon, and they were content to wait and see how the case of the first consignment that came in would be decided.

FINAL EFFORT TO PROCURE A CLEARANCE
FOR THE SHIP

Under these circumstances, the committee proposed to go to the commissioners of the customs and demand a clearance, and if it were refused, then to enter a formal protest, and go and demand a pass for the ship from the governor. If he should refuse, the last hope of an amicable solution of the difficulty would disappear, and it would then be time to consider at once what ulterior measures should be pursued.

The people made this plan known to Mr. Rotch, and demanded of him to proceed at once in carrying it into effect. He was very reluctant to take such a step as to demand a pass from the governor, but the committee brought so heavy a pressure upon him that he was compelled to yield.

The twentieth day—the last one of the period allowed for discharging the tea—would come on Thursday, the 16th of December. On Tuesday, the 14th, Mr. Rotch, accompanied by a committee of ten of the principal citizens as witnesses, went to the collector of the customs to make a formal and final demand for a clearance for the vessel.

The collector on receiving the demand said that he could not give an answer until the next morning.

The committee concluded to grant this delay.

At ten o'clock the next morning, Mr. Rotch, accompanied by the ten witnesses, went again to the custom-house and asked for the answer. They were met there by the principal officers of the establishment, who informed them that they had come to a decision, unequivocally and finally, not to give any clearance to the ship until she should have discharged the teas.

The news of this result spread rapidly through the town, and greatly increased the excitement.

Preparations were made for a mass meeting on the morning of the following day—the last of the days of grace.

MASS-MEETING ON THE LAST DAY

The meeting assembled at an early hour. The committee appointed to accompany Mr. Rotch reported that the custom-house authorities had absolutely refused a clearance.

The meeting then resolved that Mr. Rotch should make a formal protest against this decision, under the usual legal forms, and then at once proceed to call upon Governor Hutchinson and demand a pass, in virtue of his superior authority as governor of the province. The meeting then adjourned until three o'clock in the afternoon, to allow time for these steps to be taken.

THE AFTERNOON MEETING

When the vast assembly, the most numerous, it is said, that had ever been held in Boston, came together in the afternoon, Mr. Rotch did not appear. It was stated, however, that he had made his protest, and had gone in search of the governor, but found that he had left town. The governor had gone out to his country seat in Milton, probably on purpose to be out of the way.

Governor Hutchinson

Hutchinson had spent his life in seeking to deserve and secure the favor of the English ministry by aiding them in every way to extend and establish the control of the mother country over the colonies—in hopes that in the end he might be rewarded by being made a British peer; which is the usual recompense of those who have rendered distinguished services to the party in power. But in order the more successfully to accomplish this very end it was necessary that he should do as little as possible to impair his influence over his countrymen in America. So he worked a great deal secretly and in the dark, and while in America he seemed very friendly to the cause of his countrymen, he wrote private letters to England denouncing their proceedings and their leaders. Thus while he was secretly acting in the interest of the British government, he avoided every occasion for doing anything openly to displease the people of the province.

Accordingly, though he was determined not to give a pass to the vessel, in this case, he wished very much to avoid the odium of refusing one, and so he attempted to keep himself out of the way.

Mr. Rotch, however, was conveyed by post with great speed to Milton, found the governor, and compelled him to take his stand. Thus brought to the necessity of choosing, the governor seems to have concluded it to be best for him to run the risk of offending his countrymen, rather than to displease the English ministry, and endanger his expected peerage. He refused the pass.

Mr. Rotch made all haste back to the meeting in order to report the result.

The Meeting in the Evening

He did not get back till nearly six. The meeting house had been dimly lighted for nearly an hour, with lamps and candles such as could be brought in. During the interval which had elapsed, speeches had been made, all of the most decided and determined character—but still all presenting the most serious and solemn views of the impending crisis.

When at length Mr. Rotch made his appearance, and gave in his report that the governor refused to grant a pass, the venerable

Samuel Adams arose and said that he did not see that that meeting could do anything more to save the country.

Sudden Breaking up of the Meeting

It seems that this result had been fully anticipated, and the arrangements for immediate action had all been previously made. For no sooner had Mr. Adams uttered those words, than a yell like the war whoop of an Indian was heard in one of the galleries, and was answered by similar cries at the door. The meeting was of course thrown at once into a state of great excitement and confusion. The man in the gallery was observed to be disguised as an Indian, as were also those at the doors. In the midst of the confusion voices were heard crying,

"To Griffin's Wharf! to Griffin's Wharf! Boston Harbor for a teapot tonight!"

Amidst these and similar shouts and cries the people crowded to the doors and passed out into the street, and vast numbers of them, following the Indians, poured through the streets in a torrent in the direction of the wharf.

Many persons were not content to go as spectators. They ran into shops on the way, blackened their faces hastily with soot or charcoal, turned their caps inside out, and covered their shoulders with old blankets or anything else that they could lay their hands upon.

Even those who had prepared themselves beforehand, were very imperfectly, but yet very oddly disguised. They had discolored their faces in various ways, stuck feathers into their hats and caps, clothed themselves in old frocks, gowns, red woolen caps, and wore various pieces of stuff as substitutes for blankets over their shoulders. Many of them were armed with hatchets and axes.

Numbers of people joined the party without assuming any disguise at all.

Destruction of the Tea

As soon as the party arrived at the wharf, they set a strong guard to prevent being interrupted, and then immediately took possession of the three vessels—which it will be recollected, had all been brought to Griffin's Wharf—and commenced at once the work of hoisting up the chests of tea, breaking them open, and pouring the contents over the side into the sea.

They went to their work in a very deliberate and systematic manner, it seems, for before going on board the vessels they divided themselves regularly into three parties, with a captain, and also a boatswain—whose business it was to give the necessary calls and signals for lowering and hoisting—for each vessel.

In one of the vessels—and the proceedings were much the same in the others—the captain of the party on going on board, sent a man down into the cabin to the mate, who was the officer in command, to ask politely for a few lights and the keys of the hatches, in order, as he said, that they might do as little damage to the vessel as possible.

The mate at once gave up the keys, and also sent his cabin-boy to procure a bunch of candles which, when obtained, were immediately put in use, and the work was begun.

The crews of the vessels did not in any case attempt to make any resistance. In fact several of the sailors assisted in hoisting the chests up from the hold.

It was estimated that there were nearly a hundred and fifty persons engaged in the work, only the principal leaders, twenty or twenty-five in all, being disguised. They worked industriously, but so great was the quantity of tea—three hundred and forty chests in all—that it took three hours to hoist up and dispose of the whole.

Of course, during the operation, a great deal of tea was spilled upon the decks and trampled underfoot, and it seems that some of the party conceived the idea that there would be no sin in their gathering up a portion of this waste, to carry home as a present to their wives or mothers, or to preserve as a souvenir of the transaction. Such attempts were favored by the obscurity of the night, notwithstanding the light of the moon, and of the candles that were flaring here and there about the decks and on the bulwarks.

But these attempts did not succeed. All suspicious movements of this kind were closely watched, and several persons who had succeeded in filling their pockets were seized and very roughly handled. Some of them had the portion of their clothes containing the pocket, or the recess, which had been filled with tea, cut or torn away without any ceremony, and thrown into the water, that all might go together out to sea.

Thus the work of destruction was accomplished in the most thorough manner. The next morning, it is said, a long line of tea was seen floating in the water, extending from the wharves down the harbor toward the castle, as it was slowly carried away by the tide.

The excitement continued for several days, and in all the towns along the shores of the harbor, and for some distance into the interior, a close watch was kept for tea which might, by any possibility, either of accident or design, have been saved; and in several instances, parcels and packages to which suspicion attached were seized by the people and publicly destroyed.

CHAPTER IX
THE BOSTON PORT BILL

EXCITEMENT IN ENGLAND

The destruction of the tea in Boston harbor, as related in the last chapter, took place about the middle of December, 1773. Very full accounts of the affair, as well as of all the preliminary proceedings, which were of such a nature as in some degree to implicate the whole population of Boston and vicinity in the act, reached England early in the spring, and of course produced a very profound sensation. The ministry were filled with resentment and indignation, and the national pride even among the people, was aroused, and began to assume a very decided attitude.

"Can it be possible," thought they, "that the inhabitants of a petty provincial town, three thousand miles removed from all the rest of the civilized world, can seriously think of braving and resisting the power of the British empire?"

THE PORT BILL

The ministry very soon resolved upon a series of measures for punishing the town of Boston for the audacious act of which it had been guilty, and reducing the province to subordination.

The measure intended for the punishment of Boston was the closing of the port entirely, by forbidding the entrance of any ships from the sea, and also the removal of the legislature, the courts, and all the public business of the province of every kind away from the town. The measure would thus operate to suspend, and if long enough continued, to destroy the commerce, and so far as possible, all the business of the town, and consequently to deprive the mass of the people of all possible means of gaining a livelihood.

In order to introduce this measure with sufficient solemnity, the ministers drew up a message to be sent by the king to Parliament, giving Parliament formal and official notice of the destruction of the tea, and calling upon that body to adopt at once such vigorous measures as the occasion demanded for maintaining the authority of the government and the majesty of the laws.

About a week afterward, they brought forward in Parliament a bill embodying the first of the series of measures which they proposed to adopt, which was the closing of the port of Boston, and without any serious difficulty carried it through both houses.

In all such cases as these it must be understood that although in form the king calls upon his Parliament to adopt such measures as in their wisdom they judge the case requires, and Parliament in response to the call, frame and pass the bill, it is really the ministry that act, since they draw up and put into the hands of his majesty the call, and they also frame and carry through the bill. Thus both the call and the response are their work, though it is still true—and this is a very important consideration—that they cannot do this work without having the deliberate sanction and approval of the king for one portion of it, and of Parliament for the other.

PERIOD DURING WHICH THE HARBOR OF BOSTON WAS TO REMAIN CLOSED

The bill provided that the harbor should remain closed during the pleasure of the king—that is, of the king in *form,* but of the ministers in fact. In other words, although Parliament closed the port, they gave the ministers authority to open it again, in the name of the king, whenever they should be satisfied that the end sought for had been attained.

The ministers declared plainly what would satisfy them and induce them to open the port again. What they should require, they said, was first, that the people of Boston should make compensation for the tea that had been destroyed—and secondly, that they should otherwise satisfy the king of their sincere purpose thereafter to render due submission to his government.

OTHER MEASURES ADOPTED FOR BRINGING THE COLONY UNDER CONTROL

The Boston Port Bill was one of a system of measures which the ministry had resolved upon adopting, to meet the emergency; for finding that the spirit of the people was in some degree aroused, they determined to avail themselves of this opportunity for effectually subduing the refractory spirit which had so long prevailed among the people, and for bringing the colony, once for all, under complete and permanent control. There were three of these measures, and they were all brought into Parliament, in rapid succession, and readily passed. The second of these three measures was an act remodeling the executive government of the colony.

REMODELING OF THE PROVINCIAL GOVERNMENT

By this second measure it was enacted that the governor's council, the members of which had hitherto been appointed by the colony, while the governor himself was appointed by the king, should themselves also henceforth be appointed by the king, and that the judges, sheriffs, and all other important executive officers should be appointed by the governor. Even the jurymen of the courts, who had hitherto been elected by the people, were now to be appointed by the sheriff, who was himself to be appointed by the governor, and the governor by the king—that is by the ministers.

Thus on this new system the ministers in England held in their hands directly or indirectly the absolute control of all the executive and judicial administration of the province, and could manage everything, even to the trial of accused persons in the courts, just as they pleased.

It was even provided that no town-meetings could be held, without a special license in writing from the royal governor, and no business transacted, or even discussed, at any meeting, unless it was especially included and specified in the license.

All these changes were, as the colonists maintained, in direct and palpable violation of the charter of the colony which had been solemnly granted and confirmed to them by the British crown—and thus constituted a divestiture of the people of the province, and a seizure by the king, of powers and privileges which his ancestors had most formally and irrevocably conferred upon them.

PROVISION FOR CONVEYING ACCUSED PERSONS OUT OF THE COLONY FOR TRIAL

The third and last of the system of measures, was an act providing that whenever any future disturbances in the province should occur, if any persons who had aided the governor, or any of the magistrates under him, to execute the laws, should be charged afterward in the colony with murder or any other capital offence, in consequence of his so aiding the magistrate, the governor should be authorized, if he thought best, to send them to any other colony, or to England for trial.

This was of course intended to make the friends and partisans of the government in America, reckless—or as the ministry would have said, resolute, in resisting, and, if necessary, firing upon the mob, in case of any future disturbances, by assuring them that, if they should be charged with crime in consequence of such action, and be in danger of being brought to punishment by the colonial authorities, they could be taken out their lands and conveyed to England, where the trial would be a mere empty ceremony.

EFFECT OF THE ANNOUNCEMENT OF THESE MEASURES IN AMERICA

The news of the enactment of these measures arrived in America some weeks before the appointed time for carrying them into execution. The effect was a general feeling of resentment and indignation, not merely in Boston and in Massachusetts, but throughout all the colonies. The measures were all denounced in unmeasured terms in public meetings, and by the press, throughout the land.

"By the first," they said, "the closing of the port of Boston, thousands of innocent persons are robbed of their livelihood for the act of a very few individuals. The second—the remodeling of the government, annihilates our chartered rights and liberties. And the third provides for the destroying of our lives with impunity."

APPOINTMENT OF A NEW GOVERNOR

The ministry were of course aware of the spirit of resistance which the announcement of these measures would necessarily arouse in America, and of the necessity of making efficient arrangements for meeting it. The first step which they adopted was to appoint a new governor in the place of Hutchinson, who was removed from office ostensibly that he might proceed to London, and give the ministry there the benefit of his experience and his knowledge of the country, and of his advice. General Gage, the commander-in-chief of the military forces in America, and at that time having his headquarters in New York, was appointed governor in his place.

This appointment was of itself a sufficient notification to the people of Massachusetts, that the government were intending to take hold of the work of reducing them to subjugation with a strong hand.

RECEPTION OF GOVERNOR GAGE IN BOSTON

The appointment of Governor Gage, however, notwithstanding the threatening attitude on the part of the British government, which it seemed to imply, was not at first objected to in Boston. Hutchinson had rendered himself so exceedingly unpopular among his countrymen, that they were glad on any terms to have him removed.

General Gage arrived in Boston by sea, from New York, about the middle of May, 1774. The people made arrangements to give him a cordial reception. He landed at Long Wharf, where great crowds assembled to welcome him, and to escort him through the streets. He made an address in which he assumed a very conciliatory and friendly tone, and spoke indulgently and apologetically of the recent disturbances—expressing the opinion that the accounts of them had been greatly exaggerated. In a word, he made a very favorable impression upon the people, and they dispersed at the close of the day with great hopes that the prospect for the future was brightening—at any rate with the determination to give the new governor a fair trial.

That night, however, a crowd of men and boys assembled, and after various other demonstrations, burnt Governor Hutchinson in effigy in the streets.

Arrival of the Intelligence of the Passage of the Port Bill

These incipient indications, however, of returning goodwill proved very transient and fallacious, for it was the same vessel that conveyed the governor to New York, which also brought in the intelligence of the passage of the Boston Port Bill, and scarcely had the ceremonies of reception been concluded before these terrible tidings were promulgated, and the people of Boston saw the ruin of the town and the poverty and distress of the great mass of the population immediately impending. The act was to go into effect on the 1st of June, and it was now the middle of May.

Effect of the Intelligence upon the Country at Large

Of course the news awakened the greatest excitement, and in many minds produced a feeling of utter consternation. The tidings were spread as rapidly as the imperfect communications and slow modes of transmission existing in those days, allowed, throughout the country. The effect of the intelligence was not to overawe or intimidate the people, but rather to increase the resentment against the government, and to make the spirit of resistance that had been rising, more concentrated and more determined than ever.

Meetings were held in the other colonies, especially in the large towns on the Atlantic seaboard, at which resolutions were passed evincing a disposition to make common cause with the people of Boston, and recommending measures for forming some kind of union or combination, by which all the colonies might cooperate in a general system of resistance. Such of the legislatures which happened to be in session at the time, began to take action looking to the same result, though the royal governors, as soon as they discovered such intentions, hastened to prevent their being carried into effect, by suddenly dissolving the assembly that entertained them. In their opinion any combination of the different colonies to resist the government of the king was treason.

The excitement thus produced in Massachusetts and throughout the country, was increased by the successive arrivals from England, bringing news of the passage through Parliament of the other enactments already specified, namely the second one, changing the system of government for the colony, with a view to the transfer of the whole executive and judicial power to the ministry in England, and the third, providing for the removal to England for trial, persons who should kill any of the colonists in attempting to put down a riot or an insurrection.

Arrival of the Fatal Day

The first of June, the appointed day at length arrived. Proclamation was made that from and after that time no vessels of any kind would be allowed to enter the harbor. Men-of-war were stationed at the mouth of the harbor to add their guns to those of the castle to enforce the order. A fortnight more, however, was allowed for vessels still remaining in the harbor to leave, after which both ingress and egress were to be alike forbidden.

The legislature was adjourned and ordered to meet next at Sale A. The courts too were appointed to be thenceforth holden there, and preparations were at once made for removing the public archives, the records of the courts and all the appointments, papers and documents of the custom-house, and all the public offices of every kind.

The people witnessed these proceedings with a mingled feeling of fierce resentment and anxious foreboding. All the business of the town, except such as could be carried on indirectly through the neighboring ports of Salem and Marblehead, was destroyed at a blow. Everybody perceived at once that this would result very soon in cutting off all means of employment and of support, from a very large portion of the community. The wealthy would be reduced to comparative poverty, for of course the rents, whether of houses, wharves or stores, and the income from almost every species of invested property must be almost annihilated—while the poorer classes whose daily bread depended on their daily labor, which in its turn depended on the daily movement of business in the town, saw absolute want, for themselves, their wives, and their little ones, closely impending.

The day was ushered in, at Boston, by tolling of the bells and by other signals and tokens of suffering and sorrow. At noon all places of business were closed, and the afternoon was devoted to various religious and other ceremonies to mark the solemnity of the occasion.

SYMPATHY OF OTHER COLONIES WITH MASSACHUSETTS

All the other colonies felt a deep sympathy with Massachusetts, and evinced an unwavering determination to make common cause with her in resisting the British encroachments on her rights. The Virginia house of representatives, or burgesses as they were called, passed a resolution, that the first of June should be set apart by the members as a day of fasting, humiliation and prayer, in order devoutly to implore the divine interposition, to avert the heavy calamity which threatened destruction to their civil rights, and the evils of a civil war—and to give them one heart and one mind firmly to oppose by all just and proper means every injury to American rights.

The royal governor of Virginia, Lord Dunmore, on hearing of the passage of this resolution, immediately dissolved the assembly, whereupon a meeting was called of the members in their private capacity, and a public declaration was drawn up and signed by them, individually, protesting that an attack made upon one of the sister colonies, to compel submission to arbitrary taxes, was an attack upon all, and must be met by the joint and united action of all.

The feeling in most of the ether colonies was substantially the same, and from all quarters the most earnest assurances of sympathy and promises of cooperation, were sent to Boston.

MATERIAL AID FOR THE PEOPLE OF BOSTON

Many of the towns were not satisfied to send mere words of encouragement. Considerable quantities of wheat and other articles of food were sent in from the interior, and several pretty large contributions in money. Some of these contributions came from a great distance. The colony of Georgia, the most remote of all, sent forward sixty-three barrels of rice, and over seven hundred dollars in money—for the relief of the sufferers.

MAGNANIMOUS CONDUCT OF SALEM AND MARBLEHEAD

The two harbors nearest to Boston were those of Salem and Marblehead, and those two towns would of course derive a considerable advantage from the closing of the port of Boston, by taking the business themselves so far as it could be transferred to other ports.

The ministry counted much upon the effect which they supposed the interests of these rival towns would produce, in fomenting divisions among the people of the colony, and preventing any earnest and general opposition to the measure. "Salem and Marblehead," thought they, "will be pleased at having the prosperity of their great rival transferred to them; and their influence, and that of the populations immediately around them will prevent any decided concert of action to resist the measure."

But they mistook entirely the spirit of the people of these towns. The people of Salem held a meeting, and addressed a memorial to Governor Gage, protesting against the shutting up of Boston, and in the course of it they said,

"By shutting up the port of Boston, some imagine that the course of trade might be turned hither, and to our benefit. But nature, in the formation of our harbor, forbids our becoming rivals in commerce with that convenient mart; and even were it otherwise, we must be lost to every idea of justice, and dead to all the feelings of humanity, could we indulge one thought of raising our fortunes on the ruins of our suffering neighbors."

The people of Marblehead offered a still more substantial proof of their firmness and magnanimity. They offered to the Boston merchants the use of their harbor, their wharves and warehouses, and even of their personal services in unloading and storing goods free of all expense.

ORGANIZATION OF A CONTINENTAL CONGRESS

The general assembly of Massachusetts, which had always been held in Boston, was removed, as has already been said, to Salem. As soon as they came together in Salem, they immediately commenced the discussion of a plan for organizing a general congress, to be composed of delegates from all the colonies, to meet at some central point and arrange measures for the common defense of the whole country against the encroachments of the home government. They commenced the transaction of this business with closed doors, knowing very well that the governor would interpose if he should in any way hear of the treasonable work which they were engaged in.

One of the members, however, who belonged to the British party, pretended to be sick, and was allowed to leave the chamber. He hastened at once to the governor, and informed him of what was going on. The governor immediately despatched a messenger with a proclamation from him dissolving the assembly. The house, however, aware of the danger of such an interruption, ordered the doorkeepers to close the doors, and to give no answer to any application for admission. The result was, that the governor's messenger knocked and summoned in vain, until the business was completed. Then he was admitted; the proclamation was received and the assembly was dissolved, after the mischief had been done.

What had been done was the passage of a resolution recommending the assembling of a congress to be composed of delegates from all the provinces at Philadelphia on the 5th of September, and the appointment of five of the most distinguished citizens of Massachusetts to attend it as delegates from that colony.

CHAPTER X
WAR

PREPARATIONS

It began now to be evident to all parties concerned, that the temper and disposition manifested on both sides were such that the contest must soon lead to open war, and both the government and the people of the colonies proceeded at once to make their preparations. General Gage began to assemble troops in Boston, bringing them in cautiously, a small body at a time, so as not too strongly to attract public attention to his movements. He experienced the greatest difficulty, however, in providing barracks or other accommodations for his men. He could not hire any existing buildings, for the owners would not let them to him, and he could not erect new ones, for the carpenters and builders, much as they were suffering for want of employment, could not be induced to work for him.

He commenced fortifying the neck of the peninsula on which Boston is situated, and which was then the only means of communication, except by boats, with the mainland; though now the waters on every side, except toward the harbor, are crossed by a multitude of long and costly bridges. General Gage's plan was to throw up a line of intrenchments across the neck, to prevent any force which might be raised in the country from gaining admission to the town. He finally succeeded in accomplishing this work, mainly through the labor of his own soldiers, for none of the laborers of Boston, or of the neighboring towns, could be found to render any aid.

OPEN RUPTURE BETWEEN GOVERNOR GAGE AND THE MASSACHUSETTS LEGISLATURE

It was in the month of June that Governor Gage dissolved the Massachusetts general assembly, as related in the last chapter. In the fall of the year he issued writs, according to the usual custom, authorizing the towns to elect members of a new assembly, which was to meet on the fifth of October. But before that time arrived the governor became alarmed at the increasing discontent of the people, and at the evident preparation that they were making for open resistance, and he accordingly issued a proclamation suspending the writs and forbidding the meeting.

The people determined to pay no attention to this proclamation. The governor had a right, they admitted, to authorize elections and appoint a time for the meeting of the assembly—and also to adjourn or dissolve it, when it had once been convened. But he had no power, they claimed, after having once issued the writs, to prevent the members from being chosen, or from coming together and organizing the assembly.

So the elections were held, and the assembly was convened at the appointed time. The governor did not appear, nor did he, as required by usage or law, send any message. The body then resolved themselves into "a provincial congress," and after regularly organizing themselves in that capacity, they proceeded to act as the legislature of the province, without paying any attention to the governor whatever.

Vigorous Measures Adopted by the Provincial Congress

The provincial congress of Massachusetts thus constituted, began at once to prepare for the impending struggle with great boldness and vigor. They appointed a committee to consider and propose a plan for the immediate defense of the province. They made arrangements for the enlistment of men to form an army. The persons thus enlisted were to be ready at a minute's warning to appear in arms. They were called *minute* men on this account. They also appointed officers to command these men, and constituted a counsel of safety to carry these arrangements into effect, and also a committee of supplies, to devise and execute proper measures for procuring the necessary military stores and munitions of war.

ATTEMPTS ON BOTH SIDES TO SECURE ARMS AND AMMUNITION

The first object which the two parties to any civil contest endeavor to attain, when they find that open hostilities are inevitable, and that the time for the commencement of them is drawing near, is to secure, each for itself, the control of all the arms and ammunition within reach. The attempts made with this view in the present case, on the one hand by the military forces of Great Britain, and on the other by the colonial authorities, led first to several bloodless military collisions, and finally to a decided battle at Lexington, in Massachusetts, and thus to the opening of the war.

The first thing done by the British government, to secure arms for themselves and deprive the colonies of the means of procuring them, was to prohibit absolutely the exportation of any arms or munitions of war from Britain to America.

As soon as news of this edict arrived in America, the people of Rhode Island immediately made arrangements for procuring arms and ammunition elsewhere. A number of people also organized themselves into a band, and seized forty pieces of cannon, the armament of a battery for the defense of the harbor, and removed them into the interior.

In New Hampshire too, a company of four hundred men were secretly organized under the leadership of a celebrated lawyer, to seize and secure the powder in the fort at Portsmouth. They succeeded in surprising the fort and taking possession of it. They made prisoners of the whole garrison and kept them confined until they had taken all the powder from the magazine and carried it away.

AFFAIR OF THE DRAWBRIDGE AT SALEM

Nor were the attempts to seize and secure munitions of war confined altogether to the Americans. General Gage, having learned by some means that the Americans had collected a quantity of military stores in or near Salem, determined to send an expedition to seize them. It would be imprudent to attempt to march the force to the spot, by land, as the people would in that case certainly give the alarm, and the stores might be removed, or a number of armed men be collected, sufficient to prevent the seizure of them.

A FORCE SENT BY WATER

Accordingly, General Gage made arrangements to send a detachment to Salem by water along the coast. The detachment consisted of a hundred and forty men. It was put under the command of Colonel Leslie. The men were embarked secretly on Saturday night, or early on Sunday morning, on board a transport, from Castle William. The vessel proceeded with them to Marblehead, where they were landed, and were then at once marched to Salem. There they learned that the stores were in the interior, in Danvers, and to reach them, there was a bridge to cross, which traversed an arm of the sea, and was fitted with a draw, to allow vessels to pass up and down. Colonel Leslie at once proceeded with his command to this bridge.

PREPARATIONS FOR OPPOSING THEIR PROGRESS

In the meantime the alarm had been given, and when the colonel reached the bridge he found the draw up, and a number of men upon the bridge beyond it. Leslie ordered these men to let down the draw. They refused to do so, and the colonel found himself quite in a dilemma. He obviously had no authority to order private citizens to let down a drawbridge, and still less any right to fire upon them, for refusing to do so, and there was apparently no other way of reaching them, except by his bullets.

Just at this moment, however, his men perceived some boats upon the shore nearby, and this at once suggested the idea of taking a party of soldiers across the water to the other end of the bridge, in order that they might let down the draw. The command was given and the men made a movement toward the boats. But before they reached them the bystanders that had collected made a rush, and with axes and clubs broke holes in the bottoms of the boats, so as to render them utterly useless.

Colonel Leslie and his men were greatly irritated and incensed at this conduct; but there was nothing that they could do. It was yet nominally a time of peace, and soldiers in time of peace could not shoot down private citizens for destroying their own boats.

By this time, although it was Sunday and most of the people were away from their homes, at meeting, as they called it, still a great many persons had been drawn to the spot, and their numbers had been rapidly increasing. Many of them brought with them such arms as they found ready at band, and they began soon to assume something like a military organization, under the leadership of a prominent man among them, Colonel Pickering. The parties thus stood face to face, at opposite ends of the bridge, and on the adjacent shores, and a conflict seemed every moment impending. Colonel Leslie demanded that the people should let down the bridge, while Colonel Pickering and those with him refused to do so.

A Compromise

While things were in this state, the Rev. Mr. Barnard, one of the ministers of Salem, who it seems had followed his congregation to the scene of the difficulty, interposed between the two parties, and succeeded after a little time in effecting a compromise—one, however, which, though intended as a salvo to the military honor of the troops, must have been anything but gratifying to Colonel Leslie and his soldiers. The colonel absolutely refused to turn back without first crossing the bridge. It was wholly incompatible with his ideas of the honor of the flag that a British military expedition should be headed off and repulsed by a mob of civilians, in an attempt to cross a river. He insisted absolutely on passing the bridge—but that being done he was willing, he said, to abandon the expedition, and return to his vessel at Marblehead.

To this Colonel Pickering and those with him agreed. They allowed to the troops thirty paces beyond the bridge, as the limit of their advance on the other side. They measured and marked this distance, and took their station beyond it, and then the bridge was let down.

Colonel Leslie marched his troops over, and then immediately returned across the bridge, and marched back to Marblehead. It is difficult, however, to understand how a British officer could find

Arrest of the Danvers expedition.

any relief from the mortification of his discomfiture, by so vain and empty an indulgence as this, which the negotiations of the minister procured for him.

THE BATTLE OF LEXINGTON

The next attempt made by the military to seize the munitions of war held in store by the colony, led to much more serious consequences. It resulted in a battle between the troops and the people, which continued in one form or another for several hours, and was accompanied with a serious loss of life, and which was the commencement of open war. This conflict was the celebrated battle of Lexington.

The stores in question were at Concord, a town about twenty miles to the north-westward of Boston. General Gage organized a force of about eight hundred men to go out and seize them. The arrangements were made on the eighteenth of April, and the expedition was to be sent off that night, at midnight in boats—for there were then no bridges connecting the peninsula, on which Boston is built, with the mainland. Every precaution was taken to keep the intended movement a profound secret, in order to prevent the people of the country from taking the alarm and either removing the stores, or making arrangements for defending them.

THE SECRET DISCOVERED

The Americans, however, in some way discovered what was going on, and early in the evening they sent two men in a boat across the water to alarm the people. The names of these men were Paul Revere and William Dawes.

The consequence was that when the British troops began to draw near to Lexington, which was the first town that came in their way on the road to Concord, they heard drums beating and bells ringing, and when they entered the village they found there about a hundred men drawn up on the green to oppose them.

THE RESULT

After a short skirmish during which eight of their number were killed, the Americans dispersed, and concealed themselves in the woods and among the houses as well as they could, while the British resumed their march to Concord. They found, however, that the alarm had preceded them, and a large portion of the stores had been removed.

The men and boys had hastily loaded them on teams, and then, making the oxen run, the boys running by the side of them and urging them on, they conveyed them to places of concealment in the woods. Such as there had not been time to remove, the troops destroyed, and then, after some skirmishing with the Americans, in which several were killed, they set out on their return.

THE TROOPS GREATLY HARASSED ON
THEIR RETURN

The news of what had taken place at Lexington and Concord spread like wildfire among all the neighboring towns, and the people everywhere seized their arms, organized themselves into companies, and hastened to the line of the road which the troops must take in returning, to intercept and harass them on their march. They fired at them from behind trees and stone walls, and lay in ambush for them at every turn.

They followed them up so closely as not to allow them a moment's rest, and worried them with so galling and incessant a fire that they became in the end almost entirely exhausted; and indeed, it was thought that they would have been entirely cut off and the whole body captured if General Gage had not sent out a strong force to meet and rescue them. By the assistance of this force they succeeded in getting back to Charlestown, though with a loss of nearly a quarter of their number.

THE RESULT

The battle of Lexington was the commencement of open war. The history of the military operations which ensued, and which resulted in the establishment of American Independence, will form the subject of the next volume of this series.

THE END.